MW01153444

AT
LAST
SHE
STOOD

There once lived a woman named Josefina Guerrero. Everyone called her Joey.

We know many things about her. We know she was a spy. We know she was an orphan. We know she was a devout Catholic who grew up in the Philippines, was confined in leprosariums for much of her life, and died in the United States. We know she was less than five feet tall and fewer than one hundred pounds, yet tough enough to cross battlefields as bullets rained around her. We know she walked through a dangerous jungle with a secret map strapped to her back, even as she suffered the debilitating effects of Hansen's disease.

We know many things about her.

Unfortunately, there are many things we *don't* know. Important things, like the names of her parents or how they died, the name of her brother, what life was like on her grandparents' coconut farm, or how she felt about leaving her young daughter behind when she came to the United States to receive treatment for her disease.

Our days are filled with big moments, little details, and small happenings. Sadly, some of Joey's days are lost to us. This is partly because of Joey herself. When she grew weary of recounting her experiences during the war, her work as a spy, or her time as a confined patient, she cut her long hair, changed her name, and disappeared into a different life. When she died in 1996, her friends weren't even aware that this diminutive Filipino woman had walked through war zones, carried secret messages for the Allied Forces, or spent much of her time in forced quarantine. They were shocked to discover the truth.

Joey is no longer here to tell us about her life.

But the pieces she left behind are enough to leave us in wonder.

This is her story.

"I am just a simple,
ordinary person . . .
I did only what you or
any other would have done."

—Joey Guerrero

ERIN ENTRADA KELLY

AT LAST SHE STOOD

HOW JOEY GUERRERO SPIED, SURVIVED, AND FOUGHT FOR FREEDOM

 GREENWILLOW BOOKS
An Imprint of HarperCollinsPublishers

You will see the word "leper" in this book. Throughout history, "leper" was commonly used to describe someone with leprosy, also known as Hansen's disease. It's used in these pages within that context. It should be noted, however, that "leper" is no longer an appropriate term to describe a person with Hansen's disease (or anyone else, for that matter). It is considered disrespectful and insensitive. You will also see the word "Japs" in written correspondence from the time period. This is a racial slur and is not considered appropriate or respectful.

At Last She Stood: How Joey Guerrero Spied, Survived, and Fought for Freedom
Copyright © 2025 by Erin Entrada Kelly
Map of Joey's journey by Ryan O'Rourke
Photo credits: page vi: Joey Guerrero, circa 1950, wearing a traditional Filipino dress; page xviii: Joey Guerrero, circa 1950; page 152: Joey Guerrero, 1970. All from the permanent collection of the National Hansen's Disease Museum, Carville, Louisiana.
All rights reserved. Manufactured in Beauceville, Quebec, Canada.
No part of this book may be used or reproduced in any manner whatsoever without written permission except in the case of brief quotations embodied in critical articles and reviews. For information address HarperCollins Children's Books, a division of HarperCollins Publishers, 195 Broadway, New York, NY 10007.
www.harpercollinschildrens.com

The text of this book is set in Carre Noir Pro/Avenir LT Std. Book design by Sylvie Le Floc'h.

Library of Congress Cataloging-in-Publication Data

Names: Kelly, Erin Entrada, author.
Title: At last she stood : how Joey Guerrero spied, survived, and fought for freedom / Erin Entrada Kelly.
Description: New York, NY : Greenwillow Books, an Imprint of HarperCollins Publishers, [2025] | Includes bibliographical references and index. | Audience: Ages 8–12 | Audience: Grades 4–6 | Summary: "A biography of the legendary and inspiring Josefina 'Joey' Guerrero: World War II spy, Filipina guerrilla fighter, war hero, Medal of Freedom recipient, leprosy survivor, teacher, and peacemaker"— Provided by publisher.
Identifiers: LCCN 2024053112 (print) | LCCN 2024053113 (ebook) | ISBN 9780063218901 (hardcover) | ISBN 9780063218925 (ebook)
Subjects: LCSH: Guerrero, Josefina, 1917–1996—Juvenile literature. | Women spies—Philippines—Biography—Juvenile literature. | Spies—Philippines—Biography—Juvenile literature. | Leprosy—Patients—Philippines—Biography—Juvenile literature. | World War, 1939–1945—Underground movements—Philippines. | Guerrilla warfare—Philippines— Juvenile literature. | Philippines—History—Japanese occupation, 1942–1945—Biography.
Classification: LCC UB271.P6 K45 2025 (print) | LCC UB271.P6 (ebook) | DDC 940.54/86599092 [B]—dc23/eng/20241226
LC record available at https://lccn.loc.gov/2024053112
LC ebook record available at https://lccn.loc.gov/2024053113

25 26 27 28 29 PC/TC 10 9 8 7 6 5 4 3 2 1
First Edition

 Greenwillow Books

To Joey

CONTENTS

PART III: Fighter

✴ ✴ ✴

I went globe-trotting across the hemisphere—
In quest of gold, frankincense, and myrrh.
I traveled through many a town and city,
In curious pursuit of art and things of beauty.

At last I stood in reverent awe before a saintly man,
His frail body in raiment white,
His lean face lined and wan

to receive his blessing of peace.

—Excerpt from "Wunderlust"
by Joey Guerrero

The area of the Pacific most affected by Japanese invasions during World War II, also referred to as the Pacific Theater, 1942

University of Wisconsin–Milwaukee American Geographical Society Library

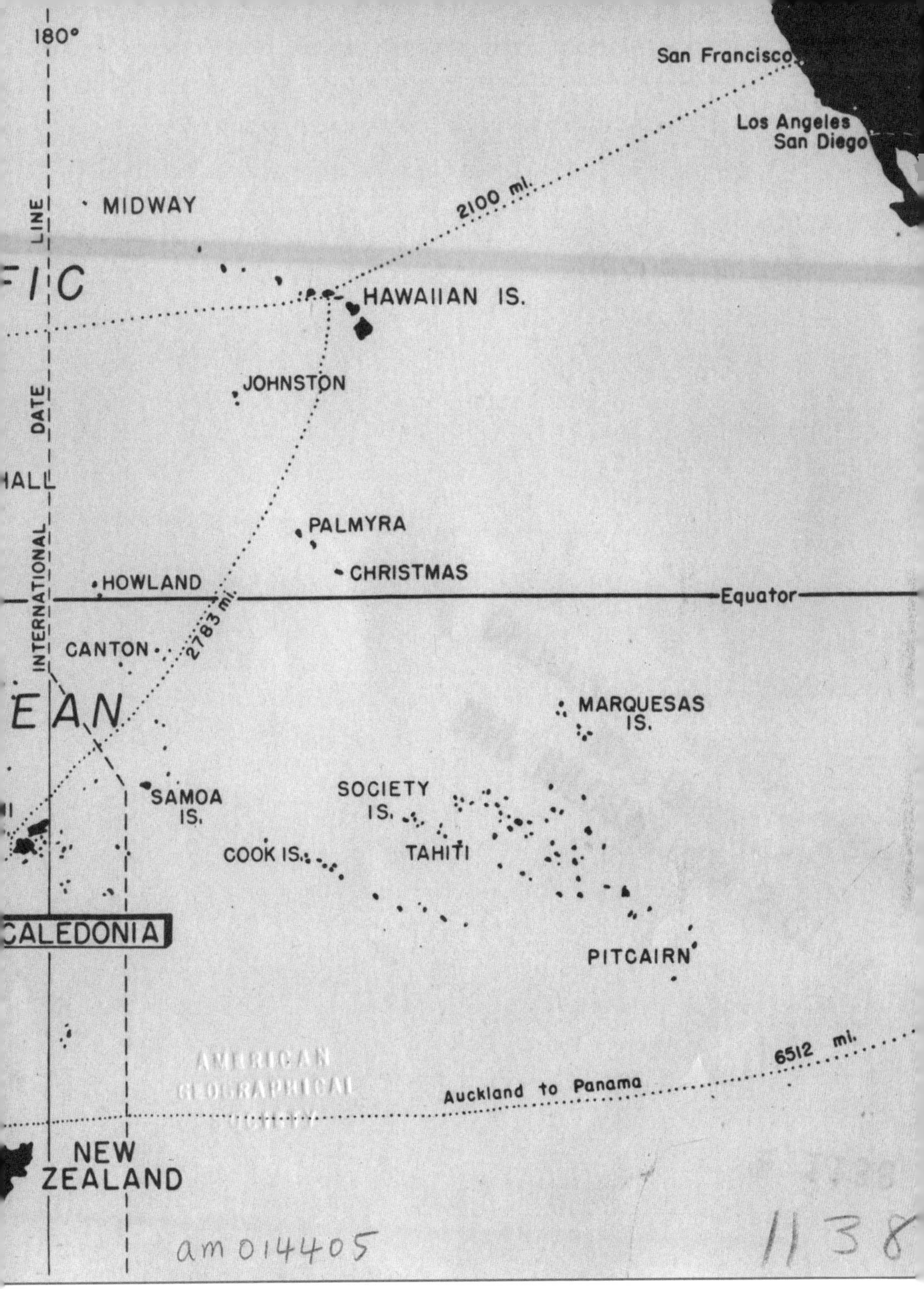

180°

LINE

MIDWAY

FIC

DATE

HALL

HAWAIIAN IS.

San Francisco

Los Angeles
San Diego

2100 ml.

JOHNSTON

INTERNATIONAL

PALMYRA

CHRISTMAS

HOWLAND

Equator

CANTON

2783 ml.

EAN

MARQUESAS
IS.

SAMOA
IS.

SOCIETY
IS.

COOK IS.

TAHITI

CALEDONIA

PITCAIRN

6512 ml.

Auckland to Panama

AMERICAN
GEOGRAPHICAL
SOCIETY

NEW
ZEALAND

am 014405

1138

PART I: Spy

*S*omewhere in a village nestled in the lush land of Lucban—a town in the Philippine Islands—a little girl is playing make-believe. Lucban is a good place for make-believe, because it is rich with legends.

On August 5, 1917, when this little girl is born, Lucban is a sparsely populated municipality with a verdant countryside, rolling waterfalls, and a historic church that has been rebuilt on the same site three times: first in 1629, then in 1733, and again in 1738. Lucban is a quiet place. Like the rest of the Philippines, it has a tropical climate, which brings high temperatures, humidity, and plenty of rainfall.

Lucban sits in the foothills of Mount Banahaw, a three-peaked volcano that many consider mystical. Some say a mythical creature beckons children to the mountain and they are never seen again. Others say there is a supernatural force inside Mount Banahaw that pulls airplanes and helicopters down from the sky. Nearby, there is a bridge that connects the towns of Lucban and Tayabas. It was built in 1854. It's said that the bridge is so strong because the building material was mixed with the blood of children.

But Josefina Veluya—the little girl playing make-believe—has stories of her own, ones where God speaks to her and tells her what to do.

She's waiting for Him now, as she steps through the dewy grass. She's not even ten years old, but she's already heard the voice of the Lord.

Well. Sort of.

That's where the make-believe comes in. She can't *really* hear God's voice booming through the trees, but she pretends she does, because she's imagining that she is Joan of Arc. Joan is one of Joey's heroes. She knows the whole story. As a teenager, Joan was visited by three saints—Michael, Catherine, and Margaret—as she worked the fields of her small village in rural France. According to the saints, God needed her help to defeat the English. By 1425, the year of Joan's first vision, England and France had been at war for decades.

What would it be like, Joey Veluya wondered, to have God speak to you directly? What would it be like to be a tiny girl in a giant war, surrounded by people who underestimated you? Joan of Arc could have hidden in her village while battles raged around her, but she didn't. She chose to fight instead. She went to war, ready to sacrifice herself for her people and her faith.

Joey wanted to be just like that. A girl who was brave, but humble. A girl who spoke out for what was right, even when people called her a witch. A girl who believed in something enough to fight for it.

Yes, that was just the kind of person Joey wanted to be.

But for now, she is just a little girl with a big imagination, stepping through the grass in the hot, humid air.

Pretending.

JOEY'S HERO: JOAN OF ARC

An engraving of
Joan of Arc
by Albert Lynch, 1903
Wikimedia Commons

When Joan of Arc was born in France in 1412, her country had been fighting England for seventy-five years. Joan, a poor peasant girl, was an unlikely candidate to change the tide of war, but when she was sixteen, she came to believe that God had chosen her to restore Charles VII to the French throne. Guided by visions of the Archangel Michael, Saint Margaret, and Saint Catherine, Joan left her village in May 1428 and traveled to the nearest French stronghold, where she asked to see Charles. The captain there did not take Joan seriously and refused to give her entry. Joan went home but returned again in January 1429. She was firm, but pious, and persuaded the captain that she was not a witch. The captain gave her permission to visit Charles in Chinon, more than three hundred miles away. Joan dressed herself in men's clothes and set off to Chinon with six men-at-arms at her side. The journey, which brought them through enemy territory, took eleven days.

Charles believed in Joan's visions. According to legend, she knew details about him that no one else did. He ordered the army to take back the city of Orléans, accompanied by Joan. She cropped her hair short like a man's and was given a suit of white armor. Joan was wounded, but she successfully helped French troops to victory in May 1429. King Charles VII was restored to the throne shortly after, with Joan at his side.

A few months later, Joan was captured by the English and held captive for more than a year. She was accused of witchcraft and the crime of dressing as a man. King Charles VII did not come to her aid. In 1431, at the age of nineteen, Joan was burned at the stake.

SPANISH COLONIALISM IN THE PHILIPPINES

The Philippines is an archipelago in the western Pacific Ocean consisting of more than seven thousand islands, many of them uninhabited. The land is rich and diverse, with mountainous country, coastal plains, jungles, river systems, lakes, and volcanic rock. The climate is tropical, with wet and dry seasons.

A shrine to Lapu Lapu on Mactan Island, Cebu, Philippines, 2013
Lowlihjeng / Dreamstime

As early as AD 1000, the islands engaged in extensive commerce with traders from China, India, the Middle East, and Southeast Asia. The people of the Philippines had their own traditions, religions, chiefdoms, and belief systems based on cultural, linguistic, and ethnic groups. No single leader ruled the islands.

That changed with the arrival of Spanish ships in March 1521. The explorers, led by Ferdinand Magellan, were searching for an easy passage to Asia from Spain.

It was not the journey they expected.

One of the ships was lost in a storm. Another deserted the flotilla and returned to Spain. Winter weather forced the men to find a safe harbor for five months, during which time there was an attempted mutiny. They had exhausted their supply of food and water, and many of them died.

Magellan was initially treated as a guest in the Philippines. Two weeks after landfall, Magellan held the country's first Mass on the island of Limasawa, located in the Visayan Islands. The Spaniards then set out to convert as many Filipinos as possible to Catholicism. The people of the Philippines practiced diverse religions at the time. Some of them worshipped nature spirits, gods of particular localities, their own ancestors, and female shamans who spoke with departed spirits and delivered prayers in song. Over time, however, Spain's collective power, influence, and force supplanted many of the local spiritual traditions, which were transformed to the Spaniards' liking.

There were those who resisted conversion, however. Tribal Chief Lapu Lapu on the island of Mactan was one of them. When Chief Lapu Lapu refused to submit, Magellan decided to take Mactan by force. Magellan underestimated the strength of Chief Lapu Lapu and his men. Chief Lapu Lapu led a rebellion, ultimately killing Magellan on April 27, 1521. He kept Magellan's body as a war trophy.

Despite Magellan's death, Spaniards continued to colonize the islands. One of them was Ruy López de Villalobos. It is believed that Villalobos is responsible for giving the Philippines its name in 1543, though it may have been a member of his crew. The Philippines is named in honor of King Philip II of Spain.

The Philippines was a Spanish colony for more than three hundred years. As a result, it is the only predominantly Christian country in Asia. Today, 79 percent of Filipinos are Catholic, making it one of the most Catholic nations in the world. Spanish influence in the Philippines is evident in the country's language, religious practices, surnames, and culture.

AMERICAN COLONIALISM
IN THE PHILIPPINES

In 1896, revolutionaries in the Philippines rose in opposition to Spanish colonial rule. The Caribbean island of Cuba, which had also been colonized by the Spanish, was fighting for independence from Spain. The violent conflict in Cuba created substantial economic and political instability, which captured the attention of the American government because Cuba was only ninety miles from the coast of Florida. When the US battleship *Maine* exploded and sank in Cuba's Havana harbor under mysterious circumstances on February 15, 1898, the US intervened. This was the beginning of the Spanish-American War. The Philippines, as a colonized territory of Spain, became embroiled in the war.

The Spanish-American War lasted less than three months, with Spain losing several land and naval battles. On December 10, 1898, Spain agreed to release the Philippines and other colonies to the United States in exchange for $20 million. This was called the Treaty of Paris.

The treaty was intensely debated by the US Senate. Those who supported the treaty believed the Philippines would serve as a doorway through which the US could gain a financial and strategic foothold in Asia, thus extending the American empire. Dissenters argued that true freedom and independence for Filipinos should be more important than American imperialism. The treaty needed fifty-six votes to pass. It received fifty-seven.

On February 4, 1899, American soldiers opened fire on Filipinos in Manila, a city on the island of Luzon. This began the Philippine-American War. Filipino guerrilla units fought for their independence, while Americans fought to colonize the islands. The war ended with an American victory in 1902 and an estimated death toll of more than four thousand Americans and sixteen thousand Filipino soldiers. It is estimated that anywhere from two hundred thousand to one million civilians died of hunger and disease.

American culture quickly dominated Philippine life. In the first years of colonization, English became the only language approved for use in school, work, or public buildings. The extent to which this eroded indigenous cultural values and traditions is still researched and debated today.

On November 15, 1935, the United States designated the Philippines as a commonwealth. A Philippine government was established with the intent to achieve full independence. This vision was thwarted by the Japanese occupation.

CHAPTER 2

At school, Joey Veluya is an athlete. She swims. She plays baseball and basketball. She is elected president of the student council. She loves classical music, reading, and writing. She especially enjoys writing poetry. Unfortunately, tragedy strikes early in her life. By the time she turns sixteen, she is an orphan. How and when her parents died is lost to history. The only certainty is that Joey is taken away from Lucban and brought to the Good Sisters Shepherd Convent orphanage in Quezon City, near the capital city of Manila. Joey, who dreams of being a nun, is a good fit for the convent. But she won't be there long.

Joey develops tuberculosis, known as TB. Tuberculosis is a feared disease during this period in history, with good reason. If left untreated, TB can be fatal. The highly contagious illness is caused by bacteria growing in the body, usually the lungs, and is spread through the air when people cough, sneeze, or spit. It only takes a few germs for someone to become infected. People with TB often suffer from a bad cough, fatigue, weight loss, chills, fever, sweats, and chest pain. Coughing up blood is another common symptom. At the time Joey contracts the disease, TB is a priority for public health leaders in the Philippines. Under the law, doctors in the

Philippines are required to report any cases of TB to authorities, including the patient's name, address, family members, and place of employment. With this information, the government keeps track of the disease, hoping to prevent its spread. Children with TB are immediately expelled from school and sent to the nearest health station. TB isn't the only reportable disease at the time. Others include smallpox, measles, cholera, meningitis, and leprosy, which is the most feared of all.

When Joey gets sick, she is uprooted once again. She leaves the Good Sisters orphanage to live on her grandmother's coconut farm in Manila. Joey doesn't have much with her when she leaves the orphanage. Just some clothes and a beloved doll. The doll is named Ah Choo. *Like a little sneeze*, she says, if you ask her.

Manila is much different from Lucban. It's a huge, bustling city with a population of more than six hundred thousand people. There are several colleges and universities, including the University of the Philippines, Instituto de Manila, and the University of Santo Tomas, the oldest university in Asia and one of the largest Catholic universities in the world. There are high-rise offices and impressive, colorful buildings, like the Metropolitan Theater, Crystal Arcade, and Jai Alai Building, a sports complex that is considered the finest art deco building in Asia. There are restaurants, shopping centers, and cinemas. The downtown mercantile district has covered walkways that link streets and buildings, providing shade and protection from rain. Jones Bridge, designed by Filipino architect Juan Arellano, stretches across the Pasig River. Its arches are adorned by sculptures representing motherhood and nationhood. There are centuries-old churches alongside bright, modern facades. Many consider Manila the "Pearl of the Orient" because of its beauty, commerce, and architecture.

*Manila Harbor prior to
World War II, circa 1925–30*
US National Archives

*The Manila Central Post Office,
designed by renowned Filipino
architect Juan Arellano, before
its destruction*
US National Archives

*Jones Bridge,
designed by
Filipino architect
Juan Arellano,
stretches across the
Pasig River in prewar
Manila, 1931.*
US National Archives

11

It is here that Joey—now cured of tuberculosis—meets Renato Guerrero. Renato is a medical student whose father is a doctor. Joey has no idea yet how influential doctors will become in her life, but she knows *this* doctor is important to her. They go on dates and realize how much they have in common. They both love art and music. They're both intelligent and curious. They're both devout Catholics. Soon, they are married. Joey is only sixteen, but she's pleased with the life that stretches before her—a road that many women have traveled before. She will be a wife. She will be a mother. She will go to Mass on Sundays.

She puts one foot in front of the other, as she always does, ready to walk that path. But the little girl who pretended to be Joan of Arc stays with her, even as she settles into wifehood, even as she embraces a life of domesticity, even when the world catches on fire all around her.

CHAPTER 3

The Philippines is rich with magical legends and folktales, but it's rich with resources too—sugar, timber, gold, tobacco, and hemp, which can be used for paper, rope, and textiles. And there are many powerful men with their eyes on the island nation's abundance of raw materials. One such man is Ishikawa Shingo, a captain in the Imperial Japanese Navy. In 1936—the same year Joey gives birth to a daughter named Cynthia—Shingo tours the Philippines and other parts of Southeast Asia.

Captain Shingo takes note of the Philippines' supply of oil, which is something the Japanese military needs if it's going to accomplish its vision. Shingo's goal, and that of many other Japanese leaders, is for Japan to control all of Asia, just as Germany wants to control all of Europe. Japan, led by Emperor Hirohito, has a mighty ally in Germany, where Nazi Party leader Adolf Hitler currently rules. Japan and Germany have similar aspirations, and similar enemies. The United States, which has occupied the Philippines since the Spanish-American War in 1898, is one of those enemies.

Japan has already increased the size of its army by the time Shingo visits the Philippines. In just a few years, it will grow by thirty combat divisions and one hundred aircraft squadrons, and its navy will be larger and stronger than the navies of the United States and Britain combined. Industries in Japan are preparing for war, and to win wars, you need raw materials. The Philippines has a lot of them, not just oil. And because of its location, the islands are immensely valuable strategically for any nation that wants to dominate the Asian coast.

It will take careful planning to invade the Philippines. The country is comprised of more than seven thousand islands, most of which are smaller than one square mile. More than sixteen million people live there. Not to mention the US military, which has bases throughout the country.

It will take careful planning, indeed, but the Japanese imperialists believe they must advance if they want to fulfill their vision.

They just need to find the right time to strike.

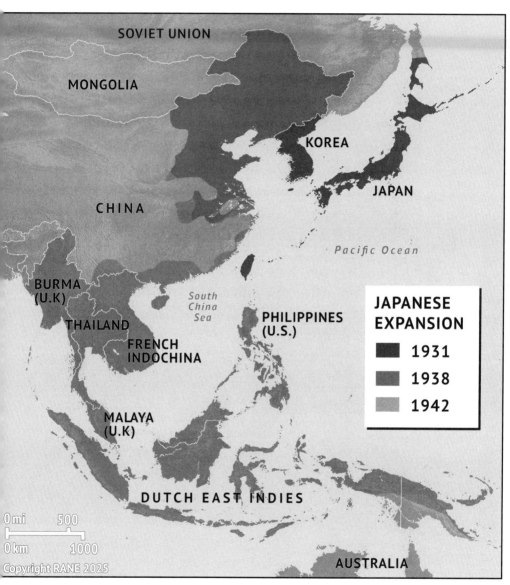

Japanese expansion from 1931 to 1942
RANE

CHAPTER 4

In 1939, Joey develops a fever.

There is never a good time to get sick, but this is a particularly bad time. Joey's little daughter, Cynthia, is only a toddler. It's difficult to care for someone else when you don't feel well, and Joey's fever is relentless. No matter what she does, it won't go away. And it's not just the fever. Joey's skin is flushed. There are red welts on her left arm and elbow. Trickles of blood dribble from her nose for no apparent reason. As soon as she thinks the nosebleeds are under control, another one is just around the corner.

Joey soldiers on, as she always does, but there is plenty to worry about. There are rumblings that Japan will soon invade the Philippines. American troops, who have occupied the islands for generations, increase their presence as the new decade approaches.

In 1940—the year Joey first notices sores and bumps, known as "lesions," on her face—the land, water, and skies around Manila are quiet. By 1941, when her feet and legs swell, whispers about an invasion grow louder. During that year, Joey's skin scales and flakes. All her joints ache.

Joey is a deeply devout Catholic, so she views her suffering through the lens of her faith. She believes, down to her aching bones, that God won't give her anything she can't handle.

If she must be sick for a while, so be it. She crawls into bed, desperate to get better, and relies on help from loved ones to care for Cynthia.

Her rest won't last long.

WHAT WAS WORLD WAR II?

World War II was a battle between two groups of countries—the Allies and the Axis. The major Allied powers were the United Kingdom, China, France, the Soviet Union or USSR (often known as Russia), and the United States. The major Axis powers were Germany, Italy, and Japan.

Germany was ruled by Adolf Hitler, leader of the Nazi Party, who wanted Germany to rule Europe. He started by invading Poland, which prompted Britain and France to declare war. By the summer of 1941, Germany had invaded Denmark, Norway, Belgium, the Netherlands, Luxembourg, France, Yugoslavia, Greece, and Russia.

Hitler didn't just want to rule Europe—he also wanted to create a so-called master race. To eliminate "racial enemies," the Nazis killed approximately six million Jews and imprisoned even more. This is known as the Holocaust. The Nazis targeted additional groups, as well—the Romani, Jehovah's Witnesses, people in the gay community, people with disabilities, Russians, Poles, political opponents, and others.

As Germany fought to dominate Europe, Italy focused on the Mediterranean region, and military leaders in Japan aimed to dominate Asia and the Pacific. Many nations in the Pacific Ocean and Southeast Asia were either ruled or occupied by Great Britain, France, the Netherlands, and the United States. Japan wanted to eliminate Western influence in the East and create a Greater East Asia, ruled by their empire.

The political ideology practiced by the Axis powers is known as fascism—a far-right, authoritarian, ultranationalist movement characterized by a dictatorial leader, militarism, and a belief in natural social hierarchies, such as "master races." Fascist governments often engage in oppressive practices, such as fraudulent elections, censorship and book bans, control of mass media, human rights violations, and the imprisonment or execution of political dissidents.

Many German, Italian, and Japanese citizens did not support the fascist practices of their governments. Dissenters were often hunted, tortured, imprisoned, or killed.

CHAPTER 5

In mid-November 1941, a group of Japanese artists and religious leaders—poets, painters, writers, photographers, and the like—are suddenly drafted into the Imperial Japanese Army.

They have no prior notice that they are wanted or needed in the national military, but they arrive at their designated stations as requested. The officials ask strange questions like "Do you know how to carry a canteen?" or "Have you ever worn a saber?" The artists who give satisfactory answers are then subjected to a simple physical examination. Those who pass the interview and exam are swiftly divided into four groups. Each group is given a secret code, though they don't know what it means or what it's for.

On November 29, the artists arrive at Chirun Port in Taiwan, which is under Japanese rule. The group consists of six novelists and poets, four painters, five cameramen, two broadcasting technicians, fourteen Catholic priests, twelve Protestant ministers, five filmmakers, and more than one hundred journalists. They still have no idea where they are headed or what they are doing there, only that they're involved in some sort of cultural military organization. They are met by Lieutenant-Colonel Katsuya Tomishige, who tells them they are part of a Propaganda Corps. Many of them aren't sure what that means.

"I don't know anything about propaganda work," Tomishige says. "It is all up to you."

The artists turn the words over in their minds. *Propaganda work.* It doesn't make sense. Why does a poet need to know how to carry a canteen? Why does an artist need to carry a saber? They aren't soldiers, after all.

On December 4, they are told they are leaving Taiwan. They'd left a life in Japan and had no idea what they were doing in Taiwan in the first place. They are ready to serve their country, certainly. But when they push off the coast with the Japanese Navy, they can't help but wonder: *Where are we going?*

THE PROPAGANDA CORPS: MIKI KIYOSHI

Miki Kiyoshi
Portraits of Modern
Japanese Historical Figures

Some members of the Propaganda Corps were enlisted as punishment for their liberal political ideas. One example is Miki Kiyoshi, a philosopher, scholar, and university professor who was active in the anti-fascist movement in Japan. In 1930, he was fired from his teaching job and briefly imprisoned for contributing money to leftist causes. He was a staunch proponent of academic freedom and highly critical of Nazi Germany and Japanese militarism. Many of his works were banned by the Japanese government. Kiyoshi served one year in the Propaganda Corps. When he returned to Japan, he was charged with sheltering a political fugitive and arrested again. He died shortly after the end of World War II at age forty-eight. It is believed that his death was the result of harsh treatment in prison.

WHAT IS PROPAGANDA?

Propaganda uses misleading, biased, or exaggerated information to promote a political cause. It is often considered a form of "thought war." Propaganda is spread through almost all forms of communication, including pamphlets, books, films, music, comics, school lessons, and so on.

The goal of the Japanese Propaganda Corps was to convince Filipinos that Japan wanted to establish peace in East Asia; that Japan had sincere intentions to create a new world order; and that the US, which had colonized the Philippines, was an enemy state. The propaganda stressed that the Philippines had no hope of surviving a fight against the Japanese, and therefore should surrender immediately. Japanese propaganda also targeted American troops who were stationed in the Philippines.

Propaganda has been used throughout history by numerous governments, including the United States. Propaganda in the US was particularly rampant in the 1950s following World War II.

Although the United States and Russia were allies during the war, their individual political might, increased world power, and differences in political ideals quickly turned them into enemies in the years after. This marked the beginning of the Cold War. Because Russia—then known as the Soviet Union—was a Communist nation, propaganda in the United States focused on anti-Communist messaging. This came to be known as the Red Scare.

The Cold War ended with the collapse of the Soviet Union in 1991.

This 1947 comic produced by the Catholic Catechetical Guild Educational Society was part of a "Red Scare" in the US that raised fears about the horrors of a Communist takeover.
Catholic Catechetical Guild Educational Society

At the end of 1941—around the time the eventual members of the Propaganda Corps first arrive for their interviews—Joey's husband, Renato, takes her to a specialist. By now, Joey's aching body is swollen. She no longer has much of an appetite. She barely has any strength.

The news isn't good.

The doctor informs them that Joey's skin lesions, never-ending fever, nosebleeds, and painful joints are caused by Hansen's disease, better known as leprosy. The doctor's voice is gentle, but Joey and Renato both understand the gravity of her diagnosis.

Throughout history, leprosy has been one of the most misunderstood, feared, and reviled diseases in the world.

In the mid-nineteenth century, for example, several people in a small Canadian village in New Brunswick developed leprosy. In response, the townspeople built log enclosures far from everyone else and forced the lepers inside. The lepers were fed through a small hole in the wall. Eventually, they became too ill to eat. When that happened, the villagers stopped feeding them altogether and let them die.

In 1937—just four years before Joey's diagnosis—lepers in the Chinese province of Guangdong were promised an allowance of ten cents. But it was a trick. When they gathered to receive their money, soldiers rushed in, bound them, and shot them all. Their bodies were thrown in trenches and burned.

Historically, there have been strict rules when it comes to lepers. In Manila, the capital city where Joey now lives, lepers were once required to wear hoods and cloaks and ring a bell to announce their presence. In some places, lepers had to yell, "Unclean!" and shake a rattle as they walked through the streets.

In this watercolor by Richard Tennant Cooper, circa 1912, people scramble to get away from a leper. In their haste, the crowd has left an infant on the roadside. The leper strolls by, ringing a bell.
History Picture Archives

At the time of Joey's diagnosis, people with leprosy are taken from their families and forced into isolation. This is true in almost every society with documented cases of Hansen's disease, from the United States to the Philippines. Many of those suffering from the disease never see or speak to their families again. People believe that the only way to keep healthy people safe is to lock lepers away. In reality, leprosy is only minimally contagious, so the risk to healthy people is low. Science shows that 95 percent of the human population has natural immunity to Hansen's disease. To catch it, you must be part of the 5 percent of the population without immunity, and you must be in prolonged physical contact with someone who is sick.

Still, the disease is a feared condition for the afflicted and non-afflicted alike. Advanced cases of leprosy can cause blindness, nerve paralysis, painful sores, and deformity.

When Joey and Renato learn of her diagnosis, these are the realities they face.

The doctor says Joey needs to be separated from Renato and their daughter, Cynthia. Even if the risk of infection is low, isolation is the foundation of all treatment, and separation from society is required by law. When they get home from the appointment, Cynthia is playing in the nursery. Joey stands back and watches. She wants to hug and kiss her daughter goodbye, but she doesn't dare.

Joey's doctor should report her to the authorities so she can be shipped off to a leprosarium. But Renato, a doctor himself, knows that Hansen's disease is marginally contagious and cannot be spread through casual contact. Joey needs good medical care, but she isn't a public health hazard. Renato knows this, and so does Joey's doctor. They arrange for someone to treat her in secret. As long as no one else knows, they are safe from public scrutiny.

As December approaches, however, they discover that they aren't safe at all.

LEPROSY

Leprosy—now known as Hansen's disease—is caused by a tiny rod-shaped germ called *Mycobacterium leprae* that enters the body through the air and quietly stews before showing its symptoms. It creates deformities on the skin, which are often prevalent on any exposed area of the body, like the face. One of the common symptoms of HD is pale or slightly red areas on the skin that have lost feeling, or loss of feeling on the hands or feet. A doctor makes the diagnosis by doing a test called a biopsy.

Unlike illnesses such as tuberculosis or flu, it can be difficult to hide an advanced case of Hansen's disease. Deformities make sufferers highly visible, and therefore subject to rampant judgment and prejudice.

Leprosy also has a complicated history because of its relationship with religion. Lepers are identified throughout Christianity and other religions as "unclean people" who are being punished for their sins. For this reason, the treatment of lepers has historically been brutal in many parts of the world.

Leprosy does not spread easily. Most people have natural

protection against the bacteria that causes HD. For unknown reasons, there are some who have little or no protection. Leprosy can only be spread after prolonged contact.

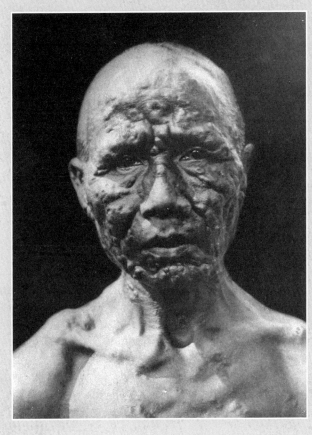

A man suffering from leprosy around the turn of the nineteenth century
History Picture Archives

Father Forbes Monaghan, a Jesuit priest from America, arrives at Ateneo de Manila University in Manila in the summer of 1940 to teach philosophy. Although he is happy to be in the Philippines, it's an uneasy year. Throughout 1941, Father Monaghan watches warily as the Americans expand their military bases and build new ones. Squadrons of airplanes fly in. The Philippine Army is called to service. Trucks and tanks rumble through the streets at night, loaded with ammunition. There are rumors of a Japanese invasion, but many people feel safe with all the additional fortifications. American officers assure Father Monaghan and others that they are more than ready to deal with Japan. Surely the Japanese wouldn't dare strike when there are so many forces waiting for them.

One morning in December 1941, Father Monaghan and other faculty members open the school for a planned exhibition. They're expecting large crowds. Not long after opening their doors, spectators arrive. Shortly afterward, however, someone rushes in and says the Japanese have bombed Pearl Harbor, an American naval base in Hawaii.

The news hits Father Monaghan like a thunderbolt—a paralyzing awareness that the Philippines is in instant, terrible danger. He prays it's a rumor. An attack on Pearl Harbor is tantamount to a declaration of war. The whispers of a Japanese invasion suddenly don't seem so unlikely; in fact, an invasion appears inevitable.

A boy rushes in with a newspaper. Crowds hurriedly gather around him. It's true—the Japanese have bombed Pearl Harbor, severely crippling US naval and air strength in the Pacific.

The exhibition crowd melts away. Telegrams pour into the university from terrified parents who want their children to come home. Students hurriedly pack their bags. By eleven o'clock that morning, the school is deserted except for the Jesuit professors. An hour later, Clark Air Base in Pampanga, an American military base on the northern shore of Manila Bay, is bombed. During the hour-long attack, nearly all of the American planes are destroyed, buildings are wrecked, and hundreds are killed and wounded. Simultaneously, a second Japanese formation raids Iba Field, forty miles west of Clark, knocking out a squadron of planes and destroying equipment. And this is only the beginning. American air power is demolished as the Japanese airstrikes continue.

The Japanese military have several reasons to attack Pearl Harbor and the Philippines in quick succession. The United States has formidable naval fleets in both places, and the Japanese want to disable those fleets as quickly as possible. They want to prevent American forces from using the Philippines as a military base, and they want to establish themselves in a strategic area where they can launch further military action against other nations in the South Pacific. And, of course, they want access to all the resources the Philippines have to offer.

That night, Father Monaghan climbs to the roof of the university's tower and looks out onto the city. There is faint starlight on the bay, which outlines the shore, ships, and buildings in the distance. From here, they look like easy targets.

CHAPTER 8

Many miles away from Ateneo de Manila University, out on the Pacific Ocean, a ship called the *President Grant* ventures into Philippine waters. It is a passenger ship, not a navy vessel. Father Fred Julien, a Jesuit priest from New York, is on board, along with many others. Father Julien is on his way to Burma (now known as Myanmar) to serve on a long-awaited mission trip, and he couldn't be more pleased. He has brought a church bell with him to give to the Our Lady of La Salette Church upon his arrival. The bell weighs a quarter of a ton.

Before Father Julien left the United States, an Army captain named Robert Jones warned him not to go. Jones said war was coming, and traveling to Southeast Asia would be dangerous. But Father Julien didn't believe him. He is determined to complete his mission trip.

Father Julien is giving Mass on board the *Grant* when the service is interrupted by an announcement. A voice comes over the public address system: "Pearl Harbor has been bombed. We are now at war with Japan."

It is too dangerous to continue the planned journey to

Burma—there is concern that the Japanese might bomb the *Grant*—so the captain changes course for Australia, with plans to dock in Manila along the way. Once they arrive in Manila, the captain tells the passengers to leave their luggage on board and find a place to stay in the city on the off chance the *Grant* is attacked while docked. In the morning, they will sail to safety in Australia. Father Julien takes his overnight bag, which contains fresh underwear, socks, and shaving supplies. He also packs his diary, which he'd started when he left the United States. He plans to document his adventures, then give it to his parents as an anniversary gift.

He leaves everything else on the ship.

With these limited belongings, he ventures into the streets of Manila to find a place to spend the night. Finally, with twilight approaching, Father Monaghan and the other leaders of Ateneo de Manila welcome him and two other men who have been stranded. Father Julien is grateful to have a place to sleep. If he must spend a night in Manila, it is comforting to be among friends.

The next morning, as soon as dawn breaks, Father Julien rushes to the harbor, anxious to continue his journey.

But there is no ship.

The *Grant* is gone.

It had been commandeered in the night by the US Navy. Someone unloaded the passengers' luggage on the dock, but most of it has been stolen. Even now, as Father Julien searches the cases and crates for his belongings, people pick through them and take what they want.

Father Julien clutches his overnight bag. He thinks of the four-hundred-pound bell, undoubtedly still on board the *Grant*, sailing farther and farther away without him.

Dejected, he returns to the university. He hopes he won't be in Manila for long, but the days turn into nights, and soon, he comes to accept that he is stranded. At the university, everyone bustles around with nervous energy. It's only a matter of time before Japanese ground forces overrun the city. Father Julien is anxious and worried.

One day he decides to go for a walk to clear his head.

Just outside the main gate, a man—filthy with mud, wearing tattered clothing—walks up to him, hand outstretched.

"Pauvre, pauvre," the man says. *Poor, poor.*

Father Julien doesn't have much. He gives the man five centavos.

"This is not enough," the man says. "My wife and children are sick. Give me more!"

Father Julien turns away, annoyed. He now has only ninety-five centavos to his name, with little hope of obtaining more. Hasn't he been generous enough? He isn't going to give this stranger all his money, not when he is in such a perilous situation himself! He'd had all his belongings stolen. He isn't supposed to be in Manila in the first place, and who knows how much longer he'll have to be there? He needs to look out for himself.

He walks off, intending to leave the man behind. Then he thinks of his brother, Ted.

What if Ted were in this stranger's position? What if Ted were covered in mud? What if Ted had threadbare clothes and had to approach people on the street with his hand outstretched? Father Julien imagines someone turning their back on his brother.

He thinks of the man's wife and children. What if he really *does* have a sick wife? What if his children are suffering right now?

Father Julien pauses, then walks back toward the gate to give the stranger the rest of his money.

CHAPTER 9

The morning after Father Julien gives all his money to a stranger, Joey rises in pain. Her condition has worsened. It has become difficult—if not impossible—to hide her illness. Her arms, legs, and face are now pocked with open sores. This is a common feature of Hansen's disease. The bacteria attack the skin in monstrous ways. At times, it can feel like your entire body is on fire. Ulcers often form on your feet. The skin thickens with lesions and lumps. The more disfigured you become, the more people look at you, step aside, and whisper to each other.

It is a painful way to exist in the world, but Joey rarely complains. Her faith never wavers. She believes that God desires this "strange hidden life," as she calls it, for her, and she doesn't question why. One day, she believes, she will find out.

For now, though, she needs to get on with her morning. She'd heard about an American Jesuit stranded at Ateneo de Manila University, and she is determined to find him.

As a devout Catholic, Joey knows all about the Jesuits, one of many religious orders within the Catholic Church.

*Joey in prayer,
July 1948*
From the permanent
collection of the
National Hansen's
Disease Museum,
Carville, Louisiana

In Catholicism, a religious order is a community of people who take solemn vows in accordance with a specific way of life. Each order reflects different ways to live those vows. The Jesuits are widely known for their focus on social justice and human rights, as well as a devotion to theology, missionary work, and education. The Jesuits are commonly associated with caring for the mistreated and marginalized. Specifically, lepers.

Joey dresses in black. She slips a veil over her shoulders, makes sure it covers her hands and arms, and sets off for the university. She doesn't want to approach the doors. Instead, she stands a distance away and studies the people coming and going, looking for the white American priest.

Finally, she sees him.

"Psst!" she calls. "Psst!"

Father Julien turns toward her.

Joey waves.

Father Julien waves back. Then he continues walking.

"Psst!" Joey calls again, beckoning him.

Father Julien hesitates, but eventually walks toward her. When he sees the black veil and pocked skin, his face pales.

"Are you Padre Julien?" Joey asks.

"I am Father Julien," he says, confused. He doesn't know any local people in Manila, besides the priests at the university and two other men from the *Grant* who'd been stranded with him. "Possibly you're looking for a Jesuit priest of the same name or a similar name," he says.

She asks again if his name is Father Julien, and if he is a La Salette priest.

"Are there not three of you stranded in my country?" she continues.

"That is correct," he says.

She reaches into the folds of her dress, produces an envelope, and hands the small package to him. He takes it cautiously, then peers inside. The package contains one hundred pesos—far more than the amount he'd given away. Father Julien gasps. He has so many questions. Where did the money come from? Who is this woman in black? How does she know his name? But when he looks up, she is gone.

Later, he asks a local Jesuit if he knows her.

"Yes," the man replies. "That is Joey Guerrero."

CHAPTER 10

When the Japanese Propaganda Corps lands in the small Filipino village of Santiago, Bauang, there are a few million leaflets onboard their battleship. Corps members have the immediate task of distributing them. They are then ordered to produce fifteen thousand more within the day, using the ship's printing press equipment. Corps members are divided by skill—writers, interpreters, and artists—and are told to develop messages that urge the town's inhabitants to come down from the nearby hills and mountains where they have sought refuge. The messages must be convincing. They promise villagers that the Japanese Army has no intention of harming them as long as they follow the rules. The leaflets are then loaded on planes and dropped across the countryside, while posters—painted by some of Japan's most talented artists—are pasted on the walls of schools, churches, and other prominent buildings. The Corps follows this pattern village by village as they move closer to the capital city of Manila, about seventy miles north of Bauang.

When they reach the city, the Corps develops plans to take control of all press, radio, and film so they can spread their message of a unified East Asia, position the United States as an enemy, and encourage Filipinos to join their cause. The Japanese military orders all newspapers to stop printing and all bookstores are searched. Any material that advocates democracy, exposes wrongdoing by the Japanese military, or contains anti-Japanese sentiment is confiscated.

The Japanese Propaganda Corps works diligently to erode the relationship between the Philippine armed forces and United States military, collectively known as the United States Army Forces in the Far East (USAFFE). They make ample use of radio broadcasts to convince Filipinos to abandon the United States. Some broadcasts feature voices of mothers appealing to their sons to come home. Others feature ex-USAFFE soldiers trying to convince Filipino soldiers to surrender immediately.

"Why do you still allow yourselves to be the slaves of the American imperialists?" one twenty-minute broadcast says. "If you have any patriotism and self-pride at all, you should leave the American Army and surrender to the Japanese who came here to assist the Philippines."

Many leaflets appeal to the Filipino soldiers' homesickness by saying that their parents, wives, and loved ones are waiting for them. The leaflets fall on the country like rain.

It is a palpable lie that the Japanese soldiers
kill prisoners of war. We have thousands of
your comrades cooperating with us.
Hold your hands up!

Examples of materials distributed by the Japanese Propaganda Corps, 1942–43
US National Archives

CHAPTER 11

Joey is no longer able to conceal her condition, so she quietly moves to Baguio, a mountain town north of Manila, to be treated by doctors in secret. Baguio is home of the Philippine Military Academy and Camp John Hay, an American base that has been overtaken by the Japanese.

December of 1941 is a brutal month for the Philippines, especially in Manila. Things have escalated quickly—and frighteningly—for Filipinos in the weeks following the Japanese Army's December 8 attack. The Japanese have effectively wiped out America's air and sea power, and the capital city is in turmoil. There are traffic jams as people desperately try to escape. Constant air raids result in casualties; hospitals are overrun, disorganized, and chaotic. Rumors run rampant—there are false reports of parachute invasions, gas attacks, and spy infiltrations. No one knows what to believe. General Douglas MacArthur, the officer in charge of the United States Army Forces in the Far East, abandons his home in Manila and relocates to the fortified island of Corregidor. There, the general establishes a new headquarters in a network of underground tunnels.

On December 26, 1941, General MacArthur declares Manila

an "open city." Essentially, this means that no military forces will actively defend it. The intent is to spare Manila from further destruction. If there is no one for the Japanese soldiers to fight, there's no need for more violence. That's the hope, anyway.

Father Monaghan watches from the university roof as the city slowly changes shape. Looters descend on the unprotected ports and set them on fire. Clouds of smoke rise from the mountains to the south and the east as Philippine demolition squads blast bridges and culverts, hoping to keep the Japanese at bay. Eighteen million dollars' worth of valuable oil are dumped into the Pasig River to keep it out of Japanese hands, but things quickly spin out of control and the oil

Manila was declared an open city in December 1941 to avoid its destruction as the Imperial Japanese Army invaded the Philippines.
US Army / Japanese Photograph

catches on fire. Father Monaghan sees and hears the explosions. He hurries off the roof, runs toward the fire, and finds a village in flames. He pushes through the smoke and ash to help villagers escape. When he's done all he can, he returns to his perch on the roof. The horizon is dotted with fire and smoke.

Japanese soldiers occupy Manila in the early months of 1942 and establish around-the-clock patrols on main thoroughfares and side streets. They continue to drop bombs on nearby airfields. When this happens, the Jesuits dive under tables or beds for protection. They emerge when the bombings are over and rush to the bomb sites to help the wounded and pray for the dead and dying. After a particularly brutal attack on Nichols Air Field, Father Julien, who should have been in Burma, encounters a tangle of bodies. He slides ankle deep in blood and intestines to anoint the dead men, asking God to be merciful.

Meanwhile, Joey monitors her health in the mountains of Baguio. Her goal is to escape the attention of authorities and wait for her health to improve. She lives a cloistered life, troubling no one. She prays. She thinks of her daughter. She thinks of her husband. She wonders what will become of her.

Her quiet life doesn't last. Someone—a doctor, presumably—reports her to the authorities.

She knows her days of freedom are numbered, so she packs her bags and flees. She decides to go back to her home in Manila. But when she gets there, Manila is not the city she remembers.

CHAPTER 12

There is another woman in Manila with a head full of worries. She's never met Joey, nor has she ever heard the name Joey Guerrero. Not yet anyway. Her name is Gertrude Hornbostel, and she can think only of Hans.

Gertrude, who everyone calls Gertie, walks the streets of Manila, stepping over one piece of propaganda after another—fliers with hand-drawn images depicting danger for dissenters, carefully worded warnings about what happens when you break the rules, even write-ups implying that all will be well, so long as no one complains—and every minute, she is reminded of Hans.

Hans is her husband. They have been married since 1913. Gertie's father didn't approve of Hans because he was enlisted in the US Marines and there were too many pitfalls to military life. Gertie's father tried to send her away, but it didn't work. She and Hans planned a secret rendezvous and got married behind her father's back. From that day on, they were virtually inseparable.

In 1922, Hans resigned from the Marine Corps and secured a position as an anthropologist. Six years later, Hans and Gertie moved to the Philippines so he could work as an advertising manager for a magazine. At the outbreak of World War II, Hans joined the US Army as a captain, working as a mining engineer. His job is to rig bridges with explosives and plant mines. It's an incredibly dangerous task, and Hans is soon captured. The Japanese military moves easily through the open city of Manila. They capture foreigners, mostly Americans. Soon, they find and capture Gertie. Because Japan and Germany are allies, Japan periodically sends prisoners to live with German families, who are sometimes called "sponsors." Gertie is given an option: She can live with a German sponsor, or she can become a prisoner of war.

She chooses prison.

Soon enough, she is carted off to the University of Santo Tomas in the heart of Manila. The university has been converted into an internment camp. Hundreds of prisoners—most of them foreign civilians, like Gertie—are held here. Each prisoner has about twenty square feet of living space. Bathrooms and supplies are scarce. Even worse, more and more people keep arriving as the Japanese military captures anyone considered an enemy. Meanwhile, planes emblazoned with the red sun and armed with missiles soar overhead. Gertie thinks of those missiles, and she thinks of Hans.

Despite the poor conditions in the internment camp, the prisoners are optimistic. The American military is mighty, after all, and will probably arrive soon to rescue them. The prisoners assume they will only be detained for a few weeks. Tops.

A Japanese Mitsubishi A6M2 war plane, a feared fighter aircraft during the war, emblazoned with the red sun symbolic of Japan
US Army

CHAPTER 13

Joey, now twenty-four years old, stands at the gate of Ateneo de Manila University in the early months of 1942. The Japanese Armed Forces have flooded into the school, looking for contraband, and she wants to warn as many people as she can. When she sees Father Julien, she stops him and whispers, "Do you have anything you shouldn't have?"

Father Julien does. "My diary," he replies.

He'd been devoted to his diary, documenting everything that he had witnessed since he left New York, including details of the Japanese invasion.

The diary is precious to him, but it is also dangerous. Besides photographs of Japanese war planes and bombings, there are stories of American soldiers who had escaped the Japanese and how the Jesuits hid the soldiers at the university, then smuggled them out in the middle of the night. This information is sure to get the Jesuits killed. Rather than leave the diary behind in his room, Father Julien carries it with him under his robes.

He has it with him now as Joey, alarmed, says, "Give it to me, quickly!"

Father Julien reaches inside his cassock for the diary, but it is too late. A Japanese military policeman grabs his collar and forces him inside where the Japanese soldiers bark orders, telling everyone to pack a bag. Only one each.

Joey disappears back into the crowd.

Father Julien quietly slips the diary out of its hiding place and puts it with his prayer book.

He isn't as careful as he thinks. A soldier snatches it up and flips through it, growing increasingly angry when he notices the photos of the Japanese planes and Father Julien's entries about the war.

Father Julien takes back his diary and turns to the first page. He shows the soldier a photo of his parents. "Do you have a Papa?" Father Julien says. "Do you have a Mama?"

The soldier glowers, mutters something in Japanese that Father Julien doesn't understand, then takes the diary back and places it on a pile of confiscated materials. If you touch it again, you will be killed, he warns.

But Father Julien suspects he'll be killed anyway if the diary makes it out of the university and the Japanese read it in its entirety. When the soldiers leave the room, he rushes past the pile of seized materials, grabs the diary, and hurries to the bathroom. He rips out all the pages and pictures, his heart thundering the whole time. He shoves the pages into the toilet and flushes. But they don't stay down. Soon, all his soggy, scribbled pages bubble up and spill all over the floor. Father Julien falls to his knees and scoops up the wet pages. He tears them into even tinier pieces and tries again.

This time, the diary pages disappear for good.

CHAPTER 14

Gertie Hornbostel and the other prisoners at the Santo Tomas internment camp are desperate for news. They thought they'd be freed within a few weeks, but the weeks have stretched into months. They try to remain hopeful, but in May 1942 they receive devastating news: Corregidor, the island where General MacArthur had established his new headquarters, has been defeated. The propagandists litter MacArthur's forces with flyers that say, in part, "You are doomed."

Gertie and the others also learn of a three-month battle on the peninsula of Bataan, which the Japanese won. Four thousand Americans and thirty thousand Filipinos were killed. Those who survived were captured. The prisoners at Bataan were told they'd be taken to San Fernando, Pampanga, in central Luzon, about sixty-five miles away. But they wouldn't be going by bus, train, or boat. They had to make the journey on foot.

The men had been fighting for three months. They were exhausted and defeated. Some of them were sick, injured, or both. But it didn't matter. They had no choice.

It came to be known as the Bataan Death March.

After the three-month Battle of Bataan, more than 75,000 American and Filipino prisoners of war were forced to walk sixty-five miles from their capture to various camps. The final death count is unknown, but it has been estimated that anywhere from 5,000 to 18,000 Filipinos and up to 650 Americans died on the journey. April 1942.
US Army

Gertie learns that Hans was part of the Bataan Death March. Thankfully, he has survived. He also survived cerebral malaria, a severe mosquito-borne illness that can cause paralysis, coma, and death. Gertie receives the news of her husband in bits and pieces. She learns that he is interned at a camp in Los Baños, nestled between Mount Makiling and Laguna de Bay. Most importantly, he is still alive.

For Gertie, each day at Santo Tomas gets a little harder. The prisoners make the best of what they have. Grown-ups craft toys for the children out of lumber, bamboo, whatever they can get their hands on. When those supplies are gone, the toys are made from scraps and old clothes. The prisoners' hopes waver as the weeks pass, but many remain optimistic that they will soon be liberated, even as others joke that they will spend the next ten years crammed together, sharing a bathroom with hundreds of other prisoners, wearing clothes that fall apart at the seams, going to sleep dreaming of their families.

Gertie keeps her spirits as high as she can. But after a few months at the internment camp, she's withered. Her weight falls to a hundred pounds, which is unusual for her. She is tired. Her body aches.

She has never been a feeble woman in any sense. When she ran away to marry Hans, for example, she'd had to escape the watchful eye of her father, sneak off on foot, and swim half a mile to their rendezvous point. She'd followed her husband to war zones. She refused the relative safety and comfort of house arrest with a German family and chose to go to prison instead.

But she is increasingly unwell.

Maybe it's all the stress, she thinks.

When the lesions appear on her skin, she knows it is something more.

CHAPTER 15

Meanwhile, Joey is in Manila, where she receives medical care in secret from a compassionate doctor. Her condition ebbs and flows. Some days, it is unbearable. Other days, she feels better. It is agonizing to be away from her daughter and husband, but this is how it is for now.

For many Filipinos, their once-familiar neighborhoods have become a strange new world. Japanese soldiers swarm the streets. There are endless rumors of bloodshed and torture. Hundreds of Filipino men have escaped into the mountains to organize their own militias.

Joey and her female friends also have to deal with unwanted advances from men, especially because Joey's house is near a Japanese military barracks. There are times when Joey simply ignores it. But on one particular afternoon, a group of Japanese soldiers harass her and a group of her friends as they walk down the street, and her temper flares.

Joey is outraged. Her strength has been inconsistent in the years since her diagnosis, but at that moment, it is back full force. She raises her umbrella at the largest soldier in the group and whacks him with it, again and again, until he and the others finally shut up and walk away.

Maybe it wasn't the smartest thing to do, to hit a brawny soldier with an umbrella. But one of the women in Joey's group takes notice and calls Joey that night.

"Come to our house," she says, and hangs up.

When Joey gets there, she is met by her friend's husband.

"A woman of your spirit should join the guerrillas," he says.

The guerrillas are small groups of Filipino combatants who work with the US military to fight the Japanese. Guerrillas aren't organized like a traditional army. Instead, they consist of armed civilians and paramilitary—unofficial military combatants who operate similarly to legitimate armed forces. Guerrillas receive funds for weapons and other resources from local families, social organizations, even the Jesuits.

Guerrilla fighters in the Philippines during World War II, January 31, 1945
US National Archives

The guerrillas live in the hills and mountains, where grass grows up to fifteen feet high, tearing clothes to shreds and cutting through the skin like razors. When it rains, clouds envelop the mountains, and the flooded valleys buzz with swarms of mosquitoes.

A Filipino man shows US soldiers his bolo knife, which he used to kill enemy combatants. A bolo is a traditional knife of the Philippines. August 7, 1945.
US National Archives

Just about everyone in the Philippines knows of the guerrilla forces. Sometimes the men come down from the mountains, demanding provisions. Sometimes the men emerge from the countryside to ambush parties of Japanese soldiers, who retaliate by killing everyone, including innocent civilians. For some, the guerrillas—who are meant to protect the people from invaders— are a frightening force themselves. Mostly, though, the guerrillas are symbols of resistance, especially after Manila is declared an open city and the Americans no longer actively defend it. Thousands of Filipinos help the guerrillas by providing intelligence and supplies. When the Japanese prohibit Filipinos from gathering in groups, churches organize resistance meetings inside chapels under the guise of worship. Secret couriers gather donations and deliver them to the guerrillas in their mountain hideouts.

The propagandists with the Imperial Japanese Army develop flyers and press releases to threaten the guerrillas, hoping to quash their spirits.

TO THE OFFICERS AND MEN OF THE FILIPINO SCOUTS, XIᵀᴴ DIVISION.

The Japanese Forces are well aware that you are attempting to continue hostilities in the mountain regions behind their backs.

If you do not cease these hostile acts immediately and surrender, the full might of the Japanese Forces will burst over your heads and you will be completely annihilated.

The whole situation is completely clear. You have not the slightest chance. Isolated actions on your part will not make the slightest difference in the outcome of these hostilities.

Surrender immediately to our superior forces and save your lives. If you do not do so, the Japanese Forces will go into action against you and will completely annihilate you. You are given herewith fair warning.

Commander-in-Chief
of the
Japanese Forces.

March , 1942.

An example of material distributed by the Japanese Propaganda Corps, March 1942
US National Archives

Filipino artist Manuel Rey Isip, who worked as an illustrator for motion pictures in New York, created this poster in 1943 at the request of Washington, DC's, Office of Special Services, Commonwealth of the Philippines. The poster was distributed to Filipino organizations in the United States and at army posts and naval stations.
US National Archives

The threats don't work on the guerrillas.

They don't work on Joey either.

She asks her friend's husband what he has in mind.

He tells her the Filipino underground is sending information about the Japanese to General Douglas MacArthur to help plan the liberation of the Philippines. "You're the kind for our secret service," he says. "Will you join us?"

Joey barely hesitates.

"I can't do big things," she says. "But every little bit helps."

Yes, he agrees.

Every little bit.

NEWS IN THE UNDERGROUND

When the Japanese military took control of all media in the Philippines, Filipinos lost access to objective news sources and were left only with propaganda. Japanese periodicals, leaflets, and pamphlets rained over the city, giving only the Japanese military's perspective on the news and events of the day. Filipinos were desperate for real news, not the sleek and skewed messaging they received from the Propaganda Corps.

Many established Filipino journalists joined the guerrillas to publish underground newspapers. They smuggled shortwave radios into the hills so they could listen to overseas reports, which they would transcribe into their articles. It's unknown how many of these papers were printed during this time, but there are at least fifty documented publications. *The Liberator* was chief among them.

Filipino journalists faced numerous challenges to publish their newspapers. It was difficult to find supplies, and once the papers were printed, it was incredibly dangerous to distribute them. If you were caught, the punishment was death. In 1943, the Japanese military raided one of *The Liberator*'s locations, destroyed their printing equipment, captured two staff members, and killed three editors. In 1944, two men were put to death when they were caught circulating copies.

The underground staff scoured the countryside for paper and other supplies and panhandled on the streets of Manila for money. On one occasion, they stole a Japanese truck and sold the parts. They used the money to keep the presses going.

Staff members went to great lengths to distribute *The Liberator* to the people. They hid copies in their underwear, in their shoes, under false bottoms in their vehicles, and in tin cans.

Guerrilla newspapers, including *The Liberator*, reported on Allied air, naval, and land victories, Japanese and Nazi losses, and new developments in the war effort—a direct contradiction to the messaging provided by the Japanese, which focused only on Allied losses and Japanese victories.

A Japanese gasoline dump burns across the waters of the Pasig River, 1945.
US National Archives

A family evacuates after the Japanese invade Manila, December 1941.
US National Archives

The Sixth Army headquarters in Calasiao, Philippines, January 1945
US National Archives

Although the Americans leave Manila in the hands of the Japanese—temporarily, at least—and the Propaganda Corps works tirelessly to disseminate their messages, the Imperial Japanese Army struggles in the first months of the occupation. They have the capital city in their grip but can't force it back to life. The banks, left without currency, are shuttered. Communication has been severed. The theaters are closed until the Japanese can replace American films with their own features. The Japanese soldiers try to position themselves as friends, but it's a daunting task; thousands of Filipino guerrillas are in the mountains, and nearly everyone in Manila has relatives or friends among them. Unsurprisingly, the Battle of Bataan does little to endear Filipinos to their occupiers. The newly imposed rules of behavior don't help either. Filipinos are instructed to bow every time they pass a Japanese guard. People zigzag through the streets to avoid them.

During those months, Father Forbes Monaghan often walks through the city in prayer. After the Japanese seize all the garbage trucks, trash collects in enormous heaps on the roadway. Access to food is increasingly difficult; one night Father Monaghan watches an elderly man lead his son through the trash, searching for scraps.

Dismayed, Father Monaghan pauses and studies the landscape. Around him, vermillion blossoms sway, the green mountains rise high in the distance, and the grass grows under his feet. The beautiful natural world of the Philippines perseveres, despite everything. Each day, Father Monaghan finds some modicum of peace in nature: the singing of morning birds, the distant crowing of roosters, the sun shining through mango trees. Inevitably, however, other sights and sounds swell—the humming of military trucks, the roar of bombers, families picking through trash, the flash of weapons and explosions at night.

Like Father Monaghan, Joey Guerrero is dismayed at what's happening in her city. But she's also determined to fight—especially when she is given her first trial assignment. She is told to study the barracks across the street from her house for twenty-four hours and document how many Japanese soldiers come and go, when, and in what direction. She is also told to provide information about their vehicles—How many pass by? What time? What kind? She is given an address and told to deliver her findings there.

Joey stands in her house behind drawn blinds and peers across the street with her notebook ready. She does what she is asked, but she makes extra notes too. Not just the soldiers' actions, but their appearance as well. Are they tired? Are they dirty, as if they'd just arrived from a battle? There could be something useful in how the soldiers appear, she thinks. It could give the guerrillas and the Americans added clues and perhaps an advantage.

There are other civilians doing similar work. Many of them are women. They study enemy troops from the relative safety of their homes and write down as much information as they can. This information is then covertly delivered to the guerrillas through safe houses, places the Japanese don't know about, where spies and combatants can stay unharmed.

At the end of twenty-four hours, Joey's notebook is full. She brings it to the designated address. The resistance fighters study what she's reported and invite her to join them. She is asked to sign an oath of secrecy and loyalty, which she does, without question.

Joey Guerrero is officially part of the underground network dedicated to defeating the Japanese.

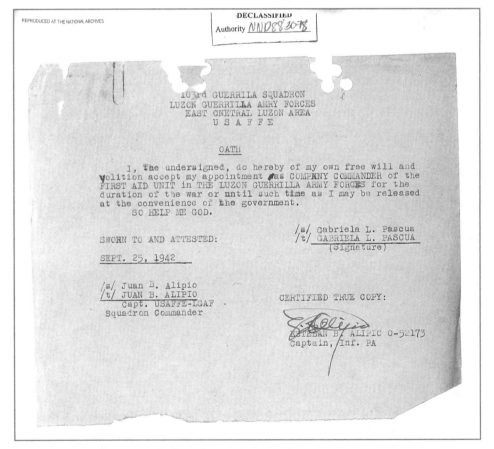

Some guerrilla groups asked members to sign an oath like this one to affirm their loyalty, September 25, 1942.
US National Archives

To: Captain Citino Lamonte
Commanding Officer
9th Co., Provincial Guards, Iloilo
Sir:

1. The present strength of the enemy on the Behia Hills, north of the poblacion of Otiles, is approximately 200.

2. This figure is arrived at by making allowances on the estimates given out by two army officers who led reconnoisance parties right into the enemy's lines.

3. Lt. Mckinto, who led a party of three, places the number of Japs at near the three century mark. In the glimmering light of the moon, Lt. Mckinto sallied forth on the underbrush to the S.W. side of the Behia Hills on Nov. 28th. With stealthy steps he crossed by the bank of the creek that winds to sitio Luego from the highest hill. There he found it swarming with slant-eyed Japs. Right there, too, his party had a frontal meeting with a Jap patrol. Caught in a dilemma of fighting it out and have the whole flock of Japs at them with death as his party's ultimate destination, Mckinto decided discretion was the better part of valor by ordering his men to roll on and on to safety. His party came off that strategy with torn clothings.

4. Lt. Sarroza, with a squad, reconnoitered on the morning of Dec. 1, on the N.E. side of the Behia Hills among the mangroves north of the Pedrena fish-pond right into the mouth of the river inlet that furnishes said fish-pond with salt water. In a clearance in front of them were three armed Japs, one of which was sitting on the ground drowsy. Further on the front, Sarroza saw plenty of Japs, pancer, with Filipino PWs, estimated at 150. With that in ado, his men fired on the drowsy Jap and another one, retreating by. They retreated helter-skelter with one of his men getting a bullet on his right forearm.

5. Pitted against this enemy are three companies of the First Battalion, namely, A Co. with Lt. Bueber commanding; B Co., Lt. Magdaluo; and D Co. under Lt. Besma, absent— totaling to a little more than 200 men.

6. Summing up the situation: The Japanese have a superiority of arms. Ours is composed of a motley group of tommies, carbines, rifles, and several MGs most of which are of Japanese construction. The morale of the boys is excellent on our side, however.

7. Lt. Sevilla, one of the junior officers of Lt. Magdaluo, in view of this situation, advises the civilians to move on further to the interior towns.

Seeing you soon, Capt. in training, I am,

Yours very respectfully,
Lt. Simaco Pellorito

(2) They were absent (?) in number this morning who gathered under the recent(?) grave near the landing field. They will not allow anybody to go near them. (?) according to their companions they have ruptured the other one. They fired twice and it was presume they kill again the other one but it is confirmed that the aviator was killed. Five tanks loaded with Japanese together with their (?) & (?) were at (?) this morning. Their knowledge re crashed plane is still unknown. For further information re above subject you can inquire from the bearer pvt Bacusa.
2. Confirm reports from Casanayan states that 27 pcs under St. Aligno deserted and reported at the (?) of Lt. Besana.
Now they are under his command.

Cpl. Pedro Baler
Incharge & 2 section
Carles Sector

Although Joey's notes are lost to history, intelligence reports like these, which were written by guerrilla scouts, have been preserved in the US National Archives, Guerrilla Unit Recognition Files, 1941–48. The report pictured above has been roughly translated.
US National Archives

CHAPTER 17

There is only so much you can observe from behind shuttered windows. If Joey wants good information, she needs to go out into the city, walk among the Japanese soldiers, and see things up close. When she is given an assignment to map out the fortifications of the Manila waterfront, she readily agrees. She will have to pass through heavily guarded areas to access the port, but no matter. The port—where ships dock, load and unload supplies, and transport raw materials—is essential to the Japanese, and a tour of the area is the only way for her to discern what they're up to.

Her friends tell her she is foolish. They say she will surely be killed.

"If I don't run risks, I won't find out anything worthwhile," she says. "All the important things are carefully watched. I have to take chances."

After Joey successfully completes her mission, her courage grows steady legs, especially now that she isn't confined to bed for months at a time. When her illness is in its quiet stages, she can move through Manila without incident. She uses these periods to her advantage.

On one occasion, the Japanese soldiers near her house invite her to an officers' party in the Engineering Building of the local university. The university is being heavily fortified by the soldiers. There is a lot to observe there—certainly much more than Joey will ever see peering through her blinds. Joey's friends tell her it is disgraceful to accept the invitation. What if someone sees her, a Filipino woman, laughing and having fun with the Japanese? But Joey can't resist the opportunity to conduct spy work up close and personal.

At the party, Joey pretends to be in awe of everything she sees. She smiles and laughs and plays the role of a naive young woman. When the officers take her and a group of other women on a tour of their fortified campus, she asks question after question, memorizing all she learns.

Eventually, one of the Japanese soldiers becomes suspicious.

"Why does that woman ask so many questions?" he asks another soldier.

A woman next to Joey nudges her and whispers, "Did you hear that officer? Look out."

Joey is nervous. Has she been too obvious? What should she do now? If she suddenly stops asking questions, the men might think they'd found her out. No, she decides, she shouldn't suddenly silence herself. Better to play up her role instead. Besides, how will she get information if she doesn't get answers?

So she asks *more* questions. Silly questions that make her look mindless. She pretends to be foolish, flighty, and immature. Just a curious girl who needs a smart soldier to tell her how the world works. Every now and then, however, she slips in a question that is meaningful.

When she sees a large opening in the ground behind the Engineering Building, she makes a mental note of the soldiers going in and out and playfully asks, "What's that?"

"That's an air-raid shelter," an officer tells her.

"May we go inside?" she asks innocently, as if she's a child ready for a big adventure.

The officer smiles. "There is nothing inside worth looking at."

Joey smiles back.

The group continues their stroll around campus and eventually reaches a corner several blocks away, where Joey sees another large hole in the ground. At that moment, a soldier emerges from it. She recognizes him immediately—she'd seen him go underground behind the Engineering Building.

It isn't an air-raid shelter.

It's a tunnel.

When she gets home that night, Joey draws pictures of everything—the fortifications, the secret tunnel, the barracks—and delivers her report to the guerrillas.

Not long after, American bombers destroy the targets she marked for them.

CHAPTER 18

By 1944, Italy—one of the three Axis powers—has surrendered, but Germany has proven much more formidable. The Nazis have overrun much of Europe and now occupy Belgium, Denmark, France, Greece, Luxembourg, Poland, the Netherlands, and Yugoslavia (now Serbia and Montenegro). The Japanese, in their own campaigns, occupy Guam, Hong Kong, the Philippines, the Dutch East Indies (now Indonesia), the Malaysian Peninsula, Singapore, Burma (now Myanmar), and Wake Island.

Then June 6, 1944, arrives.

This is known as D-Day.

The Allies combine land, air, and sea forces and plan a meticulous invasion of Normandy, France. The forces include 7,000 ships and landing craft manned by more than 195,000 naval personnel from eight countries. There are nearly 133,000 Allied troops involved. And that's just the beginning. By June 30, more than 850,000 soldiers, sailors, and airmen, 148,000 vehicles, and 570,000 tons of supplies arrive in France.

This is also the year the American military—restored and reorganized—returns to the Philippines under the command of

AT LAST SHE STOOD

General Douglas MacArthur. General MacArthur and his troops land on the shore of Leyte Island on October 20, ready to fight alongside the Filipinos to defeat the Japanese.

"People of the Philippines, I have returned," General MacArthur says.

This astonishing show of might among the Allies is the beginning of the end for Germany and Japan, though a year will pass before there are any more surrenders.

Meanwhile, Joey has become an expert at writing reports and delivering messages. She hides them in her hair. She hides them in her shoes. She hides them in her clothes.

One day, she gathers a basket of fruit and decides to hide a message inside one of them. But which one? She studies each fruit and asks herself: *If I'm stopped by the Japanese and they choose to steal from my basket, which piece would they choose?* Probably the largest, she decides. She guts the smallest one, stuffs the message inside, and sets out. A Japanese soldier stops her and studies the goods. Joey holds her breath as he reaches inside the basket. It's not uncommon for the soldiers to steal things from the Filipinos, but if he finds the message . . . Well, she doesn't want to think about that. He wraps his hand around the biggest piece of fruit and takes it, just as Joey predicted. She exhales.

Another time, she has a message hidden in her braided black hair. When she's spotted by a Japanese soldier, he draws his bayonet to frighten her, then waves her along, tugging her hair as she passes. Luckily, it's braided too tightly for the message to fall out.

Joey starts referring to herself as a "little errand boy." Eventually, though, she is needed for a much bigger task—nothing little about it.

She is contacted by Captain Manuel Colayco of the Allied Intelligence Bureau. There are rumors that the Japanese plan to slaughter the prisoners at the Santo Tomas internment camp before abandoning the city, Captain Colayco explains. American troops want to storm the camp and rescue the prisoners, but the area is littered with land mines. Land mines are weapons that are concealed underground and explode under pressure, usually when they're stepped on or driven over. If the Americans launch an attack without knowing where the land mines are, the results will be disastrous.

Fortunately, the guerrillas have a map of the minefield. It's a crude map, but it's effective. It clearly marks all the mines buried between the American Army's Thirty-Seventh Infantry Division's strategic military position and Santo Tomas. Unfortunately, the map must be taken to the Thirty-Seventh Division headquarters at Calumpit, a lowland region of winding rivers more than forty miles north of Manila. The only way to get there is a two-lane road choked with Japanese military checkpoints.

Captain Colayco makes it clear that this is a highly dangerous mission. If Joey is successful, the American and Filipino fighters will be able to liberate the prisoners at Santo Tomas. If she isn't, she will certainly be killed.

Joey doesn't hesitate.

"Just tell me where to go," she says.

Joey's first order of business is to confess her sins to a priest in case she is killed during the mission. Confession is one of the most important sacraments of the Catholic Church—a holy moment in which people can repent their wrongs.

If she dies, she wants to be right with God first.

How will Joey deliver the map? She can't just hop in a car and take off for Calumpit. Japanese soldiers thoroughly search every person and vehicle that passes through the checkpoints.

Maybe if she is just an innocent pedestrian—a tiny woman, out walking—she won't raise any eyebrows, she thinks.

Yes, it's decided. She will walk.

This creates a new question: How will she *carry* the map? It's bulky and thick and stuffed inside a large envelope—much too large to tuck inside braided hair or a shoe. It can't be put inside a knapsack because a knapsack would most certainly be searched.

There is only one option. She will have to *wear* the map somehow.

There is only one part of her body that makes sense—her back.

The guerrillas tape the package between her shoulder blades, under her clothes. It's uncomfortable. Her body screams in pain and she hasn't even begun the forty-mile journey.

She rolls a blanket to carry on her back like a knapsack. Hopefully, this will hide the lumpiness of the package. *If I am stopped*, she thinks, *maybe they'll just search the blanket and never notice anything else.* Sometimes, people are stripped naked when they are searched, but maybe—just maybe—they won't bother with that. Maybe they'll simply paw through the blanket, give her a once-over, and send her along.

There's only one way to find out.

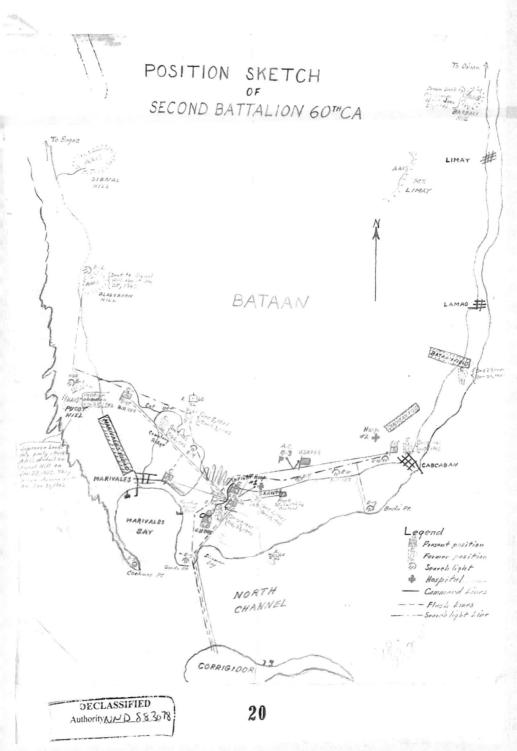

POSITION SKETCH
OF
SECOND BATTALION 60ᵀᴴ CA

BATAAN

LIMAY

LAMAO

MARIVALES

MARIVALES BAY

NORTH CHANNEL

CORRIGIDOR

Legend
Present position
Former position
Search light
Hospital
——— Command Lines
– – – Flash Lines
········· Search light Line

DECLASSIFIED
Authority NND 883078

20

Secret maps like this one, from 1942, were frequently delivered by covert couriers. Joey's map was much larger, thicker, and more detailed, making it more challenging to conceal.
US National Archives

73

CHAPTER 19

Gertie Hornbostel's life at the Santo Tomas internment camp has become a living nightmare.

When she first arrived with a few hundred prisoners, she thought it would only be weeks before the Americans rescued them. Weeks churned into months. Months stretched into years. Now, at the turn of 1945, the number of prisoners—mostly Americans, who are considered enemy civilians—has swelled to about four thousand. There isn't enough food. There isn't enough anything. There are whispers that they will all be killed soon. The rumors have a ring of truth to them—less than two months earlier, internees at a similar camp on the island of Palawan had been beaten and shot.

The situation at Santo Tomas has deteriorated at an alarming rate in the three years since Gertie's capture. Prisoners, desperate for food, catch rats and pigeons and eat them. They pull weeds out of the ground and gobble them up. Every day, someone dies of starvation. The prisoners are thin and weak. Many resemble walking skeletons. Some develop beriberi, a disease caused by malnourishment. Beriberi causes weakness, muscle loss, and confusion. Your fingers and feet tingle or lose sensitivity. Sometimes, it makes your joints swell. Every day, prisoners examine their bodies, looking for signs of beriberi.

Starvation was rampant at Santo Tomas. Male prisoners lost an average of fifty-three pounds. Nearly four hundred internees died from January 1942 to March 1945, many from malnutrition or starvation. This photo of liberated prisoners was taken on August 6, 1945.
US Army Signal Corps

Gertie is now certain that she has leprosy, and there is no medicine to ease her symptoms. There are days, however, when leprosy is the least of her concerns. It's hard to care about medicine when you don't even have food.

There seem to be fresh rumors each week. Often, the rumors dwindle to nothing. But in early 1945, a new wave of whispers travels through the camp. It's said that American and Philippine forces have landed all along the West Coast of Luzon, not far from Manila, and they will soon fight their way to Santo Tomas to liberate the camp.

But there are other whispers too.

Gertie is told that they will all be killed. A fellow prisoner saw the execution orders on the Japanese commandant's desk. The document specified that the prisoners would be lined up and shot by machine gun. If the Americans didn't rescue them soon, they wouldn't have long to live. *Perhaps we can refuse to line up*, Gertie thinks desperately. *And in the confusion, some of us can escape.*

The prisoners hope for liberation, but they know the American and Filipino troops face a tough battle ahead. The Japanese military is strong and mighty, and they can be ruthless. Gertie doesn't have to look far to see that.

Besides, the whole area is strewn with land mines.

How will their liberators survive that?

CHAPTER 20

Father Julien, the Jesuit who once mysteriously received an envelope of money from Joey, is forced into the Los Baños internment camp near Manila in 1942, around the same time Gertie is taken to Santo Tomas. Upon his arrival, he and a friend invent a game. Every time they see each other, they whisper: "They'll be back in ten days." *They* means the American military. Like Gertie, Father Julien believes he will be rescued soon. He isn't sure if it will be within ten days, but the game lifts his spirits for a time. By late 1944, however, Father Julien has abandoned the charade. Instead, he reads his prayer book and waits.

Father Julien never imagined he'd be imprisoned for three years, but he still believes the Japanese will lose. There has been talk that the Americans are on the move. He and the other internees stand in the mid-morning sunshine and watch airplanes cross the sky. They know the planes are American. They've memorized the hum of Japanese engines by now, and these planes sound different. Of this, they are certain.

Meanwhile, their meager food rations have become increasingly sparse. There are two thousand internees at Los Baños—many of them "enemy civilians," like those at Santo Tomas, where Gertie is—and they are hungry. There are days without food, or with only a cup of vegetable broth. To survive, some of the internees eat lizards, spoiled food, flowers, vines, slugs, weeds, and discarded bones. There are terrible water shortages. On lucky days when water is available, it must be boiled first, so that it doesn't make the prisoners sick.

The Los Baños internment camp is also overrun with mosquitoes, bedbugs, rats, mice, roaches, centipedes, flies, tarantulas, and snakes. Many of these creatures carry deadly diseases. Father Julien watches helplessly as people die from malaria, beriberi, skin diseases, and starvation. He prays for them all.

When 1945 arrives, the internees peer into the distance, where a soft reddish-orange glow blazes across the horizon. The skies are crowded with American planes.

Father Julien waits.

Tensions at the camp reach a fever pitch. Japanese soldiers enforce a strict seven p.m. curfew. If anyone is out past seven, they will be shot on sight. Gravediggers work overtime as January reaches its end. By now, the camp averages about five deaths per day. The number of prisoners has fallen by half.

When the calendar turns to February, Father Julien harbors a new, secret wish. His birthday is on February 20, and he prays that will be the day of their rescue. What better gift than liberation? It seems possible. The American aircraft fly over Los Baños all the time now. The guards forbid the prisoners from watching the planes, but Father Julien hears them.

But February 20 comes and goes like any other day.

Something strange is happening, though. Japanese soldiers

surround the edges of the camp with rows of machine guns and lock them into place. The guns are pointed at the spot where the prisoners line up for roll call.

Something else too: a massive ditch has been dug nearby.

Large enough to hold many bodies.

CHAPTER 21

The air is hot and humid, buzzing with mosquitoes, as Joey Guerrero sets off on her mission to deliver the map. Her leprosy has flared, and she is in incredible pain. Her head aches. Her skin swells and blisters. But she tries to focus on the road ahead. She keeps to the side of the two-lane highway that stretches north out of Manila. It's the first day of her journey, and she is soon waved down by a Japanese soldier, ordering her to stop.

Her heart thunders as he approaches. It's clear that he plans to search her. Sweat trickles down her aching back. She waits.

The soldier peers at her curiously as he moves closer. Her face is blotted, swollen, and spotted with red patches. Recognizing the signs of leprosy, the soldier backs away, terrified, without another word. Apparently, there is no way he is going to search a leper.

Joey decides it would be safer to walk at night, away from the road and watchful eyes. Traveling at night is more difficult— the path is uneven beneath her feet, there are snakes hiding in the grass, and the trees make it hard to see what's in front of her. She needs the daylight.

She also needs to be on the lookout for snipers—they are

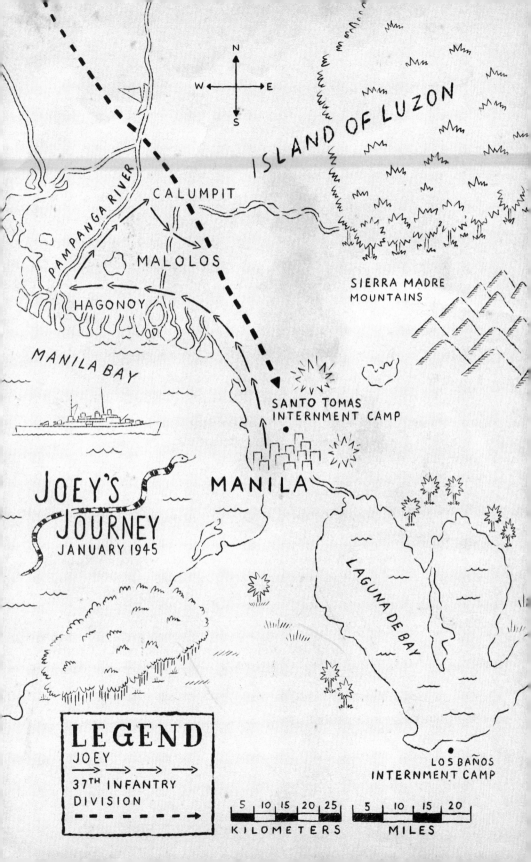

N
W E
S

ISLAND OF LUZON

PAMPANGA RIVER

CALUMPIT

MALOLOS

SIERRA MADRE MOUNTAINS

HAGONOY

MANILA BAY

SANTO TOMAS INTERNMENT CAMP

JOEY'S JOURNEY
JANUARY 1945

MANILA

LAGUNA DE BAY

LOS BAÑOS INTERNMENT CAMP

LEGEND
JOEY
37TH INFANTRY DIVISION

5 10 15 20 25
KILOMETERS

5 10 15 20
MILES

everywhere, and the Philippines offers countless hiding places for them. The thick, towering trees. The dense vegetation of the jungle.

After walking for hours and hours, she reaches the city of Malolos, a little more than halfway through her forty-mile journey to Calumpit. Her feet are bruised and blistered. She hasn't eaten, she's very sick, and there's heavy fighting up ahead, too dangerous for her to pass, either by road or through the trees. Her only option is to travel by water.

She hires a boat and captain to take her down the Pampanga River, which runs through an active combat zone and is overrun with river pirates—Filipino men on makeshift boats who hijack passing vessels by force, stealing anything they can.

Luckily, her boat is faster than the pirates, and she keeps ahead of them all the way to Hagonoy, nine miles from Calumpit, where the Thirty-Seventh Division waits for the map.

By now, Joey is truly exhausted. She's been traveling for two days and nights. Calumpit is finally within reach. But when she arrives, she learns that the Thirty-Seventh Division has relocated to Malolos.

She will have to turn around and retrace her steps.

Back through the thick trees.

Back through the mud.

Back through the combat zones and checkpoints.

Finally, she reaches the American camp, where she is brought to a man known only as "Captain Blair." It's not his real name. It's an alias, a fake name used for his protection. Joey has been using an alias too. Hers is Billy Ferrer.

"Where is the map?" Captain Blair asks.

She reveals the thick padded envelope on her back. The tape is pulled from her skin, which is sweaty, swollen, and painful. Captain Blair opens the map in front of her. It is large and detailed, revealing the positions of newly buried land mines surrounding the Santo Tomas internment camp.

"How did you get it here?" Blair asks. He offers her a plate of food—buttery pancakes with syrup—but she is too sick and tired to eat.

Joey answers simply.

"I walked," she says.

CHAPTER 22

On a February evening in 1945 at the Santo Tomas internment camp, Gertie Hornbostel and the other internees hear the rumbling of tanks, the boom of grenades, and rifle fire. Captain Colayco, the Filipino officer who sent Joey on her perilous mission to deliver the map, storms through the gates, leading the Allied Forces. The Japanese hurl grenades, one of which injures Captain Colayco. He will die from his wounds days later, but his mission is successful. An American tank breaks through the fence of the compound, followed by seven others and twenty trucks loaded with troops. Cheers from the prisoners are muffled by the sound of gunfire from the Japanese. The American tanks position themselves near the gymnasium and the Education Building.

The Japanese are taken by surprise. They rush to their trucks, which are loaded with guns and ammunition, but they don't make it in time and retreat to the safety of the buildings. Gertie hears the commandant scream panicked orders. Furniture crashes all around her as Japanese soldiers rush to barricade the building with anything they can find. When the shooting begins, Gertie falls to the floor behind two huge iron kettles. It isn't the safest spot, but Gertie finds comfort there. After three years, the end is finally near, and she knows it. They are being liberated.

She hides for hours—she isn't sure how long—listening to gunfire and shouting and explosions. At daybreak, the American and Philippine forces capture the gymnasium. Finally, just before dawn, when the sky is still dark, someone calls for the prisoners to make their way to the main building. Gertie stands and follows a circuitous route through the makeshift shantytown, dodging occasional gunfire, heading toward her freedom.

The liberation of Santo Tomas internment camp, February 6, 1945
US National Archives

At the Los Baños camp—days later and miles away—Father Julien is unnerved by the big ditch and the machine guns. He stands at the doorway of his barracks, talking to a Dutch priest, with all his worries and secret prayers tumbling around in his head. When there is a rumbling in the distant hills, both men turn toward the sound.

"I wonder what that is," the Dutch priest says.

American aircraft soar through the air. Flickers of white fall from the sky. Father Julien assumes the Americans are dropping leaflets, providing instructions or words of encouragement to the internees. But no—they aren't leaflets at all.

They're parachutes.

As soon as the paratroopers land, American fighter planes appear. They bomb the Japanese positions, pinning them high in the hills. Near the camp's main gate, a bazooka round explodes. About three hundred troops and eight hundred Filipino guerrillas charge into the camp. Father Julien and the other prisoners are trapped in the chaos. On one side of them, American paratroopers clasp rifles and fight the Japanese soldiers. On the other side are the guerrillas, doing the same thing.

Father Julien drops to the ground. Bullets fly in every direction, and he is petrified that he and his fellow prisoners will be caught in the crossfire. He frantically prays the rosary. Others join him. The exchange of gunfire and exploding grenades continues for about thirty minutes. When things finally quiet down, Father Julien pushes himself up. His legs feel like jelly, too wobbly to hold him. He has pressed his face so deeply into the pavement that gravel is embedded in his cheek.

The quiet doesn't last. New firefights flare up. Father Julien hits the dirt again and crawls toward a soiled mattress. He hides underneath the mattress and prays, prays, prays. He doesn't know how much time passes, but he finally hears a voice. He gazes up and sees an American soldier, his face covered with soot.

Father Julien is dazed. The sounds of gunfire and explosions continue. He hears the screams of the wounded and dying. The evacuations begin, starting with women, children, the elderly, and the disabled. There are fifty-nine military vehicles roaring into the camp to rescue them. The priests are among the last to leave. Father Julien boards a military vehicle. The sights around him are horrifying. He will never forget them. As he travels farther away from the camp, he thinks of all he's experienced. He thinks of the people who died. He thinks of home. He thinks of liberation.

MANUEL COLAYCO: HERO OF THE PHILIPPINES

Manuel Colayco
Eastern Montana Catholic Register

Captain Manuel Colayco was a journalist, editor, teacher, and lawyer. After the war broke out, he joined the guerrillas and became part of the Allied Intelligence Bureau. He was named commanding officer of the Manila Unit.

Captain Colayco was instrumental in the February 1945 liberation of Santo Tomas, where he once served on the faculty. He recruited Joey to deliver the map that revealed the location of land mines around Santo Tomas. After her successful mission, he joined the lead vehicle as American tanks roared toward the gates. He was well aware of the danger of leading the charge. Only the day before, he confided to a friend that he "will have the fortune of receiving the greatest honor that can be given to a solider, that of dying for his country."

When the tanks rumbled toward the university's main entrance, soldiers dismounted and crouched in columns alongside the vehicles. Captain Colayco was with them. Someone shouted "Grenade!" and the men immediately fell to the ground. Moments later, there was an explosion. Captain Colayco was wounded. He died seven days later.

Captain Colayco is celebrated as a great freedom fighter. There are monuments to him throughout the Philippines.

Manuel Colayco monument in Pasay, Philippines
Roel Balingit

Manila is an inferno as the American military storms through. Joey storms with them, through the roar of explosions, the rain of bullets, and the rat-a-tat-tat of machine guns. American soldiers huddle behind walls and in foxholes and see a tiny Filipino woman walk alone through the war-torn streets, her shoulders back as shells burst all around her. She rushes to injured soldiers and binds their wounds. If they can't walk on their own, she helps them up and guides them to safety. Then she goes back into the gunfire to look for anyone else who needs help. Sometimes, it's too late for her to do anything. When that happens, she closes the eyes of the dead and prays for them.

The Battle of Manila rages on for days, then weeks, as American and Philippine forces push the Japanese soldiers toward surrender. Joey's home is destroyed, along with everything she owns. She hides in a ruined laboratory at Ateneo de Manila University with others who have been displaced. The roof has been blasted away, so water pours in when it rains. They drink it greedily.

Father Monaghan is back at the university. He and the other Jesuits care for the refugees—people who have lost their homes—

as best they can. They gather food and distribute it, but when Joey gets her share, she gives it all away. When friends bring her clothes, she gives those away too. Finally, Father Monaghan tells her she must keep some of the items for herself. He says she is under his spiritual guidance, and he forbids her from donating anything else.

This is the only way to make sure Joey is properly fed and clothed. Father Monaghan is aware of her terrible secret—that she suffers from leprosy—and he wants to keep her as healthy as possible.

Joey doesn't seem concerned, however. She works herself to exhaustion, caring for wounded soldiers and looking after other refugees. One day, she suffers a lung hemorrhage, which causes painful coughing that produces red and frothy blood. Not to worry, she tells Father Monaghan. She isn't afraid to die. When it's her time, she will be with God. She plans to keep going until she can't anymore, and that's just what she does. When she comes back to Ateneo de Manila at night, she smells like blood and the dead.

Father Monaghan has never met anyone like Joey. He worries and prays for her, knowing her leprosy puts her in a dangerous situation. If anyone finds out about her illness, it will be difficult for the Jesuits to hide her. Her secret is safe with him, however.

As long as people don't notice she's sick, Father Monaghan should be able to protect her.

US troops carry an injured serviceman on a stretcher through the streets of Manila, February 23, 1945.
US National Archives

US troops in Manila, February 27, 1945
US Army Signal Corps

Manila was one of the most devastated capital cities in the world after the war. This legislative building was one of the finest government buildings in the East before it was destroyed, 1944.
US Army Signal Corps

THE BATTLE OF MANILA

The destruction of Manila, May 1945
US National Archives

In war, military leaders will sometimes strategically abandon all efforts to defend a city when it's clear that they will lose. When this happens, the area is declared an "open city." The hope is that opposing military forces will peacefully occupy the area, since there is no reason to fight.

General Douglas MacArthur, commander of the US Army Forces in the Far East, declared Manila an open city on December 26, 1941. The Imperial Japanese Army entered Manila on January 2, 1942. Unfortunately, it was not peaceful. They bombed the city and launched a robust propaganda campaign to convince Filipinos to submit to Japanese rule.

As the Japanese tightened their grip on the Philippines, President Franklin D. Roosevelt ordered General MacArthur to leave the Philippines and relocate to Australia so General MacArthur could regroup, strategize, and return, ready to fight. General MacArthur retreated on March 11, 1942, but promised to return. He fulfilled the promise more than two years later, on October 20, 1944.

Japanese troops fortified buildings, planted land mines, and erected tank traps in anticipation of the siege on Manila. The American cavalry arrived on February 3, 1945, reinforced by the efforts of the guerrillas. The battle was bloody. More than 11,000 buildings were leveled, including many beloved historical and cultural landmarks. More than 1,000 American troops, 16,600 Japanese troops, and 100,000 Filipinos were killed. One hundred Filipinos died for every one US soldier. Food supplies and department stores were looted. Farm equipment was stolen. Medicine vanished. The social fabric of the city unraveled. Graves were plundered in search of jewelry, dentures, eyeglasses, clothing—anything that could be sold. Starvation ran rampant.

The Battle of Manila lasted twenty-nine days, with a victory for the Philippine and US Forces declared on March 3, 1945.

Each decisive battle in Europe and the Pacific further underscored the sharp decline of the remaining Axis Powers. Germany surrendered to the Allies on May 7, 1945. Unfortunately, fighting in the Philippines would continue for several more months after the Battle of Manila; Japan would not surrender until September 2, 1945.

THE SURRENDER OF JAPAN

Filipinos and Americans celebrate the surrender of Japan, August 1945.
US National Archives

By the end of July 1945, an Allied invasion of Japan was imminent, and the Imperial Japanese Navy was incapable of conducting major operations. On August 6, 1945, the United States dropped an atomic bomb on the Japanese city of Hiroshima. The exact number of those killed is unknown, but at least sixty thousand innocent civilians—likely many more—died instantly. On August 9, the United States dropped an atomic bomb on Nagasaki, which killed at least forty thousand people. The total death toll climbed over the following months as civilians suffered from radiation poisoning and injury. The final number is estimated at more than two hundred thousand.

Japan surrendered on September 2, 1945.

CHAPTER 24

There is a hospital near Ateneo de Manila University. One day, one of the doctor's daughters shares a secret with her father: Her friend, Joey Guerrero, has leprosy.

Joey soon learns that her condition has been revealed and the doctor has contacted the authorities, which means they will be on their way to take her to a leprosarium. Panicked, Joey contacts Father Monaghan, who immediately rushes to help her.

Father Monaghan moves swiftly to get Joey out of Ateneo de Manila and into hiding. They enlist the help of a friendly American sergeant, who allows them to slip away. Father Monaghan takes Joey to the family of Lulu Reyes, a former debutante who has embarked on her own dangerous missions for the liberation of the Philippines.

Unfortunately, the Reyes family are refugees as well. Their home has been destroyed and they're moving to Ateneo, which has become a sanctuary for the displaced, in five days. This means Joey has less than a week to plan her next move. While she's with Lulu, however, she's welcomed like a beloved friend. They hug Joey and treat her like a member of the family, all while working up a plan for Joey's future. Without a place to hide Joey, there is only one option: the Tala Leprosarium in nearby Novaliches, on the outskirts of Manila.

Neither Joey nor Father Monaghan has ever been to Tala, but they don't have high expectations, especially now, as World War II comes to an end and the country struggles to provide even basic resources for its citizens. It will be a long and difficult struggle to get the Philippines back on its feet. People with leprosy weren't a high priority before; they certainly won't be now.

"Novaliches—I keep repeating the word to myself," Joey tells him. "At first, it had a horrible sound. By forcing myself to repeat it, I am getting used to it. It is like the taste for olives. You have to cultivate it. Who knows? I may eventually come to like the thought of Novaliches."

With only two days left to go before the Reyes family leaves, it seems there is no other option. Father Monaghan decides to make a trip to Novaliches without Joey.

He wants to see it with his own eyes so he can tell her what to expect. Who knows? Perhaps she will come to like the place, as she said. Perhaps it is possible.

The Tala Leprosarium is tucked in the wilderness. When Father Monaghan steps out of his car and explores the colony, he's immediately horrified by what he sees. There are ten leaking cabins, one main building, a run-down open-air chapel, and very few resources or supplies. The lepers, as they are called, are given a weekly ration of food that's half of what they need, and they are forced to cook it themselves, even in their weak and sickened conditions. Their cabins have no running water, so they trek barefoot to the main building to fetch their own. Often, they use the same water for washing, laundry, and drinking. There is no plumbing, only outhouses.

The stench is overwhelming. There is no disinfectant to heal wounds and there aren't enough bandages, so the patients wander the property with open sores, which ooze and smell. The leprosarium is funded by the government, but there isn't enough money to hire staff or purchase basic supplies, especially after the ravages of war. There aren't enough beds. There isn't enough medicine. It's overcrowded. The patients—already snatched from their families, suffering from illness, and physically and emotionally exhausted—live in filth and squalor.

As Father Monaghan casts his eyes over Tala, he thinks of something Joey once told him.

"There is pity for every other disease," Joey had said. "There are foundations for the study of cancer and tuberculosis, but for three thousand years lepers have been the outcast. Men flee from them and will not help them."

Father Monaghan is heartbroken.

Joey is right.

LULU REYES

It's unknown how and when Joey and Lourdes "Lulu" Reyes became friends. It's possible they knew each other as teenagers. It's also possible that their friendship developed while they both fought for the liberation of the Philippines.

Before the war, Lulu was a socialite in Philippines high society.

She was the granddaughter of a provincial governor and the daughter of a highly respected attorney and judge. She was often featured in the society pages of newspapers and magazines, attending balls and galas.

Lulu didn't limit her life to parties, however. She was also devoutly religious and devoted to charitable causes. She was instrumental in establishing the Girl Scouts of the Philippines. She served as president of a Catholic religious organization and worked as a volunteer for the Red Cross.

When Lulu's brother, Guillermo "Willy" Reyes, was captured by the Japanese, she vowed to find him.

It was not an empty promise.

Lulu learned that Willy had been in the Bataan Death March but had no idea whether he survived or not. Rather than sit and wait for news, she traveled to Japanese prison camps searching for him. She finally found her brother, wounded and malnourished, at Camp O'Donnell in Capas, a US military base north of Manila that was occupied by the Japanese military.

It was forbidden to enter the prison camp, but Lulu persuaded a Japanese commandant to let her see her brother. Over the course of her subsequent visits, she secretly smuggled food, medicine, money, and letters into the camp—not just for her brother, but for other prisoners too—under threat of death. One of the most important items she smuggled into the camp was medicine for malaria, which saved many prisoners' lives.

In December 1944, Lulu assembled a truckload of rice, beans, sugar, peanuts, canned goods, salted fish, and candies for the prisoners of the Los Baños internment camp. Friends told her that she'd never make it inside, but she went anyway. When she arrived, she served glasses of brandy and cordial to the Japanese soldiers and gave them Christmas gifts. Once they were adequately charmed, she kindly asked if she could enter the camp and give food to the prisoners. Once inside, she distributed the food, but also smuggled in notes and messages.

Later, the Reyes family home was destroyed in the Battle of Manila and the family was forced to flee on foot. As Lulu ran from the bombs, she passed three small children, bawling and barefoot, standing next to their parents' bodies. Lulu went back for them and delivered the children to safety.

Lulu Reyes received the US Medal of Freedom twice, on August 11, 1947, and on September 24, 1947.

CHAPTER 25

When Father Monaghan returns to Manila, he tells Joey about everything he saw at the Tala Leprosarium.

"God must have some special work for you to do among those poor forsaken creatures," he says. "If He is taking from you all the support and society of mankind, it is because He means to replace it with an infinitely stronger and sweeter intimacy with Him."

Joey is devout; she certainly believes that God has a plan for her. Still, she doesn't want to go to Novaliches—especially after what Father Monaghan has told her about Tala. She prays about it. She turns the word over and over, hoping she can find comfort in it somehow. *Novaliches. Novaliches. Novaliches.*

Father Monaghan knows of Joey's devotion to her faith. This is a woman who had wanted to be a nun once upon a time, who had pretended to be Joan of Arc.

"Consider," Father Monaghan says, "that you are going to an austere cloister, a Carmel, where Christ awaits you."

The Carmelites are another Catholic order, like the Jesuits. They live in seclusion and solitude and are revered for their self-discipline and abstention from all forms of indulgence. The Carmelites are cloistered—they do not leave their monasteries unless it's essential. Instead, they spend their time in prayer. Father Monaghan hopes that comparing Tala to a Carmelite monastery will calm Joey, make the leprosarium feel familiar to her, as if it serves a greater, more divine purpose, but deep down, he fears what awaits her.

Joey prays and prepares herself as best she can. She has very few belongings, but she has managed to keep her little doll Ah Choo through it all. There isn't much to do except take the few things she owns, get into the car with Father Monaghan and Lulu, and go to Novaliches. The friends laugh and joke the whole way, despite their destination. When they arrive at Tala Leprosarium, Joey studies the crowded, run-down cabins where she will be forced to live. She sees what Father Monaghan saw. Later in life, Father Monaghan would say that he hoped to never see a place like Tala again. But for now, he stands next to Joey and gives her a blessing.

Father Monaghan and Lulu spend the afternoon with Joey. That night, they say goodbye. When they get into the car to leave, Joey smiles and waves farewell. Father Monaghan watches her until she's out of sight. He and Lulu don't speak much on the way home.

What is there to say?

PART II: Survivor

Tala Leprosarium is located in the isolated foothills of the Sierra Madre mountains on 1,500 acres of rich, rolling land and sloped terrain. The colony itself is a cluster of leaking shacks with more than six hundred patients shoved inside. There is virtually no medical care. The patients walk the colony with bare and blistered feet. Many of them sleep crowded on the floor. Flies and mosquitoes forever buzz around them.

World War II is over, but Joey faces new battles now.

At Tala, people die of starvation and malnutrition. During the rainy season, Joey and the other patients huddle in the corners of the overcrowded cabins to escape the water, which pools on the floor and rots the wood. There isn't a single decent bed. Every available mattress is dirty, rickety, and sagging.

There are no lights. There is no running water. There are children, but no toys. No recreation for the adults either. Joey quickly realizes the people of Tala aren't really living. They are waiting to die.

There must be more to life than this, she thinks.

Soon after she arrives, Joey starts gathering everyone together on Sunday afternoons to tell stories and sing songs. She writes to friends and asks if someone can send her a guitar, ukulele, mandolin, banjo—any instrument will do. She longs for music. Joey imagines what it would be like to hear Brahms, her favorite. She thinks of how comforted the patients would be if they could hear something, anything. She dreams of games like chess, Ping-Pong, badminton, or checkers. She's desperate to read and would love to get her hands on books, comics, or newspapers. She writes to anyone she can think of who might be able to help.

When she can, Joey teaches the children what she knows so they can get some form of education. Her own daughter, Cynthia, is never far from her mind.

Although the patients at Tala are segregated from the rest of society and aren't allowed to leave, Joey is visited by her Jesuit friends. One afternoon, a priest named Father Luis Torralba comes to see her. He tells her about an American named Marie Dachauer, who lives in Sacramento, California. Marie is founding a Catholic organization called Friends of the Lepers.

"Marie is interested in helping lepers all over the world," Father Torralba explains. "Perhaps you should write her a letter."

Joey doesn't want to ask for charity from a stranger, but Father Torralba insists.

Yes, she decides. She will write Marie Dachauer a letter.

CHAPTER 27

One week later, in August 1945, Joey sits in front of a clean sheet of paper. "Dear Miss Marie," she writes.

Father Torralba encouraged Joey to tell Marie Dachauer all about Tala, and that's just what Joey does.

"Father says I must tell you everything, but the inside story of the life of the leper in a poor and sadly abandoned leper colony is too full of heartaches, misery, and want," she writes. "Many are the times I feel that it is truly an imposition to ask even my own friends to venture out here into this no-man's land, but my little girl's heart always wins out by the thought that this is what friends are for: that I may turn to them in times of stress, that I may unburden to them the weight of the cross that lies heavy at times in my heart."

Joey confesses in her letter that she has moments of unspeakable loneliness, though she finds comfort in her faith, believing that God has specifically chosen this "strange hidden life" for her.

"The thought keeps me forever joyous and young in heart," she writes. "But my companions are not so easily led." She explains that the other patients at Tala are understandably bitter, apathetic, and emotionally and spiritually broken. Joey wants to bring some form of light to them, whatever that may be.

"I desire so much to be able to alleviate all this human misery, and wish, at least, to instill once more the feeling of hope and make their lives once more wholesome and brighter. But I am only one of them and segregated and isolated. Of myself, I can really do nothing. I need your help."

Joey describes the ramshackle cabins, the lack of food and medicine, the rotted roofs and floors. She tells Marie Dachauer how much she wishes they had music or toys or any games to play.

"We are in need of a true friend," she writes. She apologizes for any imposition, since she and Marie Dachauer are strangers. Joey invites Marie to visit Tala so she can see the colony for herself. She also hopes Marie can tour other parts of the Philippines.

"Someday I hope you will come to our lovely country," she writes. She admits that some of that beauty has been ravaged by war—in fact, Manila, once the Pearl of the Orient, has been virtually demolished—"but the countryside is still verdant and green after the rains. Some of it is still very lovely, anyway."

The letter continues for three pages. She thanks Marie in advance for anything she does, even if all she does is read the letter.

"Perhaps you will be our fairy godmother," she says.

CHAPTER 28

Joey sends her letter off to Marie Dachauer in August 1945. Then she gets to work.

She scrubs the floors and sinks. She builds coffins with any materials she can find so the dead can have a decent burial, rather than being thrown into pits in the ground. She prays with the other patients. When her husband and daughter visit, she puts on a cheerful demeanor, even when she's desperately ill. She collects books—any books she can get her hands on. She reads voraciously, not just to herself, but to others. One day, a patient gives birth at Tala, and Joey helps deliver the baby. She serves almost every role she can at the makeshift church too—she reads burial prayers for the dead, she rings the bells, she teaches the principles of the Catholic faith.

Joey is more than a patient. She's a beacon. She rallies the other patients and tells them that they don't deserve to be treated this way.

All the while, she keeps writing letters.

She writes to Friends of the Lepers.

She writes to the United Nations Relief and Rehabilitation Administration.

She writes to the daughter of Manuel Quezon, former president of the Philippines.

Eventually, someone listens. A. H. Lacson, a journalist for *The Manila Times* and former guerrilla scout, makes a trip to Tala Leprosarium to see things for himself. He publishes a series of articles, in which he describes Tala as a "graveyard of the living dead." There are 650 patients and only four nurses, he writes. Most patients sleep on dirty floors and there's a constant shortage of food, medicine, and clean water. Each week, patients are given one and a half cups of rice, two pounds of meat, six pieces of fish, and three tablespoons of sugar, and they have to cook the food themselves in discarded cans over fire. About six patients die every month—not from leprosy, but from malnutrition.

"Isolated as they are from the rest of the world, these lepers have not altogether lost faith in human kindness. There is one among them who has shown thoughtfulness for her fellow sufferers and has consistently maintained the last frail link to faith in humanity, that they could not help holding onto it like drowning persons," Lacson writes.

He's talking about Joey Guerrero, of course.

"Finding life suddenly unkind to her, [she] clings to the idea that she is not entirely unwanted," Lacson continues. "There, with her, are people who need charity and she never lets a chance to alleviate their suffering go past her. The children, in particular, look up to her."

National dignitaries, social welfare workers, and government investigators descend on the leprosarium after reading A. H. Lacson's articles. They want to find ways to improve the conditions at Tala.

The wheels of change finally start to turn.

CHAPTER 29

By September 1947, things have improved at Tala Leprosarium. The cottages are more orderly. There are more social activities, including a cooperative farm. There is also a permanent chaplain.

Unfortunately, Joey's health remains unpredictable. She has bouts of fever and open sores. She's constantly tired and exhausted. She desperately wishes she could be well.

"There is so much to do, so many things to accomplish and time is short," she writes to Dr. Leo Eloesser, a surgeon from San Francisco. Dr. Eloesser had traveled the world with the United Nations Relief and Rehabilitation Administration. He met Joey during a stopover at Tala, and they became fast friends. Dr. Eloesser specializes in tuberculosis, but Joey takes every opportunity to educate him about Hansen's disease. She hopes he will decide to switch specialties and study leprosy instead.

"Perhaps you, in your great interest for the sufferings of others, might find the solution to the cure," she says.

Although Dr. Eloesser never shifts specialties, he soon joins the international cohort of Joey's supporters, which seems to grow with each passing month.

In the years since she first wrote to Marie Dachauer, politicians, journalists, and activists have learned about Joey's missions during the war and have worked diligently to get her the recognition she deserves and bring her to America so she can get treatment at the National Leprosarium of the United States in the small town of Carville, Louisiana. The hospital—known simply as "Carville"—is the only institution in the US for leprosy patients. It is considered one of the best facilities in the world for the treatment of Hansen's disease. Joey's supporters include Friends of the Lepers, American soldiers, even congressmen. Joey is convinced that Carville is her only hope for a cure, but at times it seems like an impossible dream. It is not easy to travel from the Philippines to the United States, especially when you have a mandatory quarantinable disease and require approval from Philippine health officials, the US Surgeon General, and the surgeons general of every state you will pass through, to travel.

"If I can achieve a cure, it will mean so much to my fellow patients everywhere, for I can become a sort of symbol, a symbol for hope and greater courage," she says in a letter to Dr. Eloesser. "I believe in miracles and God will see that I am cured."

If it is meant to be, she says, it will happen.

On May 29, 1948, Joey puts on a dress, brushes her hair, and walks to the open-air chapel at Tala. Nearly a thousand leprosy patients have gathered on this warm Saturday, and they're all waiting for her. She steps onto a stage and stands between Major General George Moore, an officer of the US Army who served as a commander during the Battle of Bataan, and Archbishop Francis Cardinal Spellman, a high-ranking representative of the Catholic Church who is visiting the Philippines from New York.

General Moore reads a citation, then presents Joey with the Medal of Freedom with Silver Palm, a commendation given by President Harry S. Truman to honor civilians who demonstrated incredible courage during the war. It is the highest honor a civilian can receive from the US government. Joey's friend Lulu Reyes received the same medal the year before.

General Moore tells the crowd of attendees that Joey showed "more courage than that of a soldier on the field of battle."

Archbishop Spellman has a medal for Joey too—the eponymous Spellman Medal, given to those who show great "Christian fortitude and concern for fellow sufferers."

The medals are pinned on Joey's dress.

She cherishes them deeply.

Joey with the Medal of Freedom with Silver Palm and the Spellman Medal, July 1948

From the permanent collection of the National Hansen's Disease Museum, Carville, Louisiana

CHAPTER 30

An abandoned sugar plantation on the marshy banks of the Mississippi River seems an unlikely place for a world-class hospital, but that's exactly where Carville began. In the beginning, in 1894, it was called the Louisiana Leper Home. The facility was founded and managed by the Daughters of Charity, a Catholic order dedicated to caring for the sick and disadvantaged.

The first seven patients—five men and two women—arrived by barge on the Mississippi River in the middle of the night. Carville would eventually become a world leader in the treatment of Hansen's disease, but you wouldn't have guessed it during those early years. The patients stayed in cabins that once housed the enslaved, while the nuns slept and worked in the main house. None of the facilities were adequate for anyone, much less people who were being treated for a serious illness. The buildings were falling apart. As the patient population grew, services and accommodations became even more inadequate. There was no clean water. Patients walked long distances to the outhouse and developed ulcers—oozing, open sores that become progressively worse if left untreated—on their feet. They had to haul water hundreds of yards from the river in wheelbarrows. The grounds of the plantation were dilapidated, muddy, and overgrown. The brutal south Louisiana weather— hot and unbearably humid—kept the soil wet and soggy, an ideal atmosphere for one of nature's deadliest creatures: the mosquito. One of the nuns met an untimely death in those early days, but not from leprosy. She died of malaria, a mosquito-borne illness.

The patients were not only deprived of basic needs; they were also deprived of their identities. When people arrived at Carville, they had to assume new names to spare their relatives the shame of having a leper in the family. Because of this, few patients could share even basic information about themselves. Most of Carville's patients lived under pseudonyms.

The facilities only worsened as more patients arrived, crowding the cabins. There wasn't enough staff, food, or medicine to adequately care for any of them.

As issues mounted, patients began to escape—mostly through holes in the barbed-wire fence—and the nuns were forced to report them to authorities. When captured, the patients were confined to a jail on the premises.

It was an unmanageable situation, but the Daughters of Charity were relentless in their efforts to make Carville a clean, respectable, and renowned site for the treatment of leprosy.

In 1902, the sisters marched into the Board of Control, the governing body for the home, and demanded more funds. When the Board refused, the nuns threatened to go to the newspapers. It worked. The Louisiana Leper Home received more funds, with which the nuns built a water treatment plant and new cottages for the patients.

U.S.Marine Hospital. Carville

Carville
US Public Health Service

By the 1940s, Carville is one of the leading leprosariums in the world. It isn't a perfect place, but the conditions are luxurious compared to Tala. In many ways, Carville resembles a small Louisiana town. There are about 450 patients, each with an individual room. Carville has its own post office, school, bank, store, library, and golf course. There's a lake for fishing. There are two churches. Carville also has its own cemetery.

Although Carville has several things in common with other Louisiana towns, there are marked differences, both positive and negative. The patients at Carville are effectively prisoners—they aren't allowed to leave without permission—but in some ways,

Carville is more progressive than other southern communities. At the height of racial segregation, Carville is remarkably diverse. Asians, Hispanics, whites, and Blacks work, pray, study, and play together and are paid the same salary for doing the same work at the compound. In the late 1940s, as Joey fights to make her way to the United States, Louisiana is ruled by racist policies and practices. Everything is segregated by law—drinking fountains, buses, public accommodations, schools. But at Carville, people of all ethnicities and social classes—from the destitute to the wealthy—intermingle. It is a "cross-section of the all the world's races and nationalities," as patient Stanley Stein describes it.

For years, all mail at Carville was fumigated and thoroughly disinfected by state law. Patient mail was routinely sterilized in an oven and heated for one hour at 130 degrees before leaving the facility. Because Hansen's disease is incredibly difficult to contract and can only be passed through prolonged contact, these precautions were unnecessary and useless.
Photo by the author

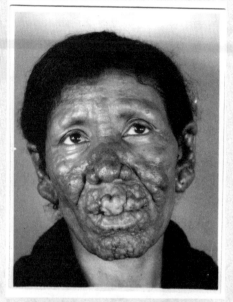
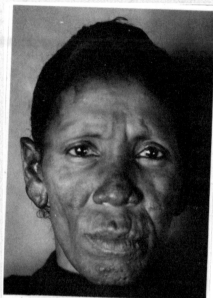

Carville's reputation as one of the top hospitals for the treatment of Hansen's disease is demonstrated in these photos. The top left depicts a patient as she first entered in 1940. The last photo was taken in 1947. The patient was treated with a new antibiotic called Promin, first used at Carville.

From the permanent collection of the National Hansen's Disease Museum, Carville, Louisiana

JOHN EARLY

John Early in his quarantine tent, 1909
Munsey's Magazine

John Early, a veteran of the Spanish-American War, arrived at Carville in 1918, when patients were treated as prisoners and pariahs rather than people who needed medical care. They were legally prevented from leaving the premises upon threat of arrest. Men and women were segregated and could not communicate without permission. Patients had no telephone. They were not allowed to vote. Parents lost custody of their children. There were strict daily rules. No games past eight o'clock, bedtime at ten. Patients who committed offenses faced isolation, confinement, and hard labor.

John Early was one of Carville's most notorious escapees. He was first diagnosed in Washington, DC, in 1908, when his face became so inflamed that his eyes were nearly swollen shut. His skin burned and itched severely. After his examination, doctors kept him in a locked room, fearing he had leprosy. When the diagnosis was confirmed, he was forcibly quarantined in a hastily erected tent in a marsh along the Potomac River. He was eventually moved to a ramshackle house on a muddy dead-end road.

Government officials had no idea what to do with Early, so they sent him to Port Townsend, Washington, to serve as a caretaker for another leper. In May 1914, he escaped. Upon his recapture, he was confined to the ramshackle house again so authorities could keep a closer eye on him. He remained there until 1918, when he was moved to Carville.

Early escaped Carville four times in his first two years. He was captured and jailed each time. After serving a thirteen-month sentence, he escaped yet again—this time, seeking refuge at his family's home in the remote mountains of North Carolina. When authorities found him, he was hiding in the bushes with a shotgun. His family, all armed, said they were willing to take care of him and keep him isolated. The standoff lasted two hours. Early was arrested and returned to Carville to serve an additional six months.

Early died in Carville in 1934 at the age of sixty-four.

CHAPTER 31

In June 1948, Joey Guerrero finally receives permission from the US government to travel to the Carville Leprosarium in Louisiana.

Everything she owns fits inside a paper bag, which she carries with her as she boards the USS *General John Pope*, a US Navy ship, in Manila. She is finally sailing to America. The letters, prayers, and newspaper articles have led to this moment—a voyage across the Pacific Ocean to San Francisco, California, where she is greeted by throngs of soldiers, reporters, and well-wishers, all of whom want to welcome her and thank her for her service.

From California, she takes a flight to New Orleans, Louisiana. She doesn't feel well on the plane. *I'm a better sailor than flier*, she thinks.

In New Orleans, she gets much-needed rest at the Covent of the Sacred Heart for several days before continuing to Carville. While there, she writes a letter to Dr. Frederick Johansen, the medical officer in charge at Carville, to let him know she is in Louisiana and will arrive soon.

"I know I shall like it here," she says of Louisiana. "Everything is peaceful and beautiful. From my window I can hear the quiet hum

Joey is greeted by doctors, soldiers, and priests upon her arrival in San Francisco, July 1948.
Associated Press

of traffic. I have a big room all to myself with a private bath. Luxury indeed! Everyone seems kind and very good. The nuns are gentle and talk in soft voices."

After a week in New Orleans, Joey climbs into an ambulance to make the short road trip to her new home.

The ambulance has windows. She lowers one of them. A rush of wind brushes her cheeks. That makes her feel better. She studies the strange world outside. The streets of New Orleans are quiet and lined with rows of neat houses, manicured lawns, and flowered gardens; it all whizzes past as the night shifts to dawn. She clutches her bag, which holds her doll, Ah Choo. Joey has been through a lot since she held Ah Choo for the first time. She is no longer a little girl. She's seen enough misery to last a lifetime.

But she won't think about that now.

She won't think about her illness or the war or the soldiers who lived and died. She won't think about what's been left in the Philippines, including her daughter and husband. She will only focus on this moment. The vast expanse of the Mississippi River. The rumble of road that leads to Carville.

I am finally here, she thinks, and she is happy to leave it at that. Besides, she only plans to stay a short while. Two years, maybe. Once she's cured, she'll return to the Philippines and reunite with Cynthia and the children of Tala. When she thinks of it in that way, it doesn't seem so bad.

She leans her head back and slowly drifts off.

This is America.

I am in America.

CHAPTER 32

When Joey opens her eyes, she sees a paved road lined with long, low buildings. A porch with tall, massive pillars looms ahead.

"Here we are, Joey," the ambulance driver says. "This is Carville."

All the fatigue from her long voyage disappears. Joey is suddenly wide awake, blinking her dark brown eyes at her new home as the ambulance comes to a stop. Someone reaches in to help her. She emerges from the ambulance to greet a group of strangers. Someone hands her red roses and ferns. Someone else snaps pictures.

"Thank you for the flowers," Joey says as everyone gathers around.

A blind man—Stanley Stein, one of the best-known figures in Carville—steps forward and says, "Welcome, Joey. Welcome to Carville." Stein, who runs a newspaper at Carville called *The Star*, has been one of Joey's most ardent supporters. Like the others on the porch of the main house, he lives at Carville under a fake name. Once upon a time, he'd been Sidney Maurice Levyson, a pharmacist from Texas.

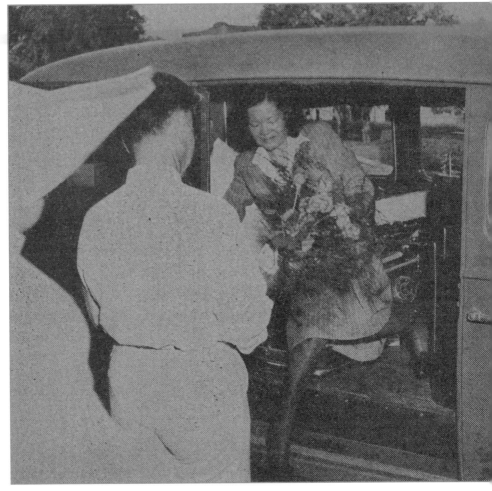

Joey arrives at Carville, July 1948.
From the permanent collection of the National Hansen's Disease Museum, Carville, Louisiana

Joey is led across the long porch. She navigates a chorus of friendly greetings as she walks down a dim, quiet corridor toward her room. When she arrives at the door, she stares at the number in front of her. She is in room thirteen. Some might consider it a bad omen, but Joey smiles. She likes the number thirteen. People are afraid of the number thirteen; they think it's unlucky. That's exactly why Joey loves it.

Room thirteen is filled with more flowers. There is a banner made of red, yellow, and blue wool that says, "Welcome Joey." Joey takes a shower and changes her clothes. Soon enough, she is propped in bed with pillows and a breakfast tray with hot coffee, warm toast, and grapefruit. She has visitors too—reporters from the New Orleans *Times-Picayune* and the Associated Press. They all want to write about the war hero's arrival. They want to celebrate the "leper spy," as she is sometimes called.

Joey answers their questions. Then everything is quiet. Joey is finally alone.

She props Ah Choo against the pillows and studies her new bed. It is wide and comfortable, with a spring mattress and cool, clean sheets. A ceiling fan whirs above her. A wall fan too. There are blinds on the window to shut out the glare of the sun. There is a dresser with a mirror, and a washbasin with running water. There is a rocking chair.

She's thirty-one but feels like an anxious child on a field trip. Throughout her life, people have often referred to her as a little girl, even in war zones, because she's so small. At this moment, that's exactly how she feels.

I'm in America, she thinks. *Look at all this luxury!*

She is happy, content, and comfortable, but another feeling twists underneath. Sadness. She thinks of the people at the Tala Leprosarium in Novaliches, who don't have beds of their own, or even clean water. The children at Tala cried when Joey left. And now, here she is, separated from Novaliches by land and sea, with warm food and a comfortable mattress and hot and cold water, available whenever she needs it.

When she lived at Tala, she often fell asleep dreaming of America, dreaming of Carville. But on this night, she thinks only of the Philippines.

CHAPTER 33

Joey Guerrero doesn't just bring a small bag of belongings to Carville—she also brings unprecedented celebrity. Her arrival in America is covered by nationwide news outlets, including *Time*, *Reader's Digest*, and all the major daily newspapers of the time. The *Fort Worth Star-Telegram* runs an editorial praising Attorney General Tom Clark, who waived immigration restrictions to give Joey passage.

Carville resident Stanley Stein, who has spent years raising awareness and advocating on behalf of those with leprosy, is thrilled with the publicity, and Joey is a powerful spokeswoman. Not only is she passionate, intelligent, and friendly, she is an unequivocal war hero. When *Time* runs an article about Joey's arrival in Louisiana, more than four thousand letters flood the offices of Carville to celebrate her arrival.

Still, there are plenty of people who aren't happy. Joey's journey sparks outrage among some Americans. One of them—signing their name only as "M. M. C."—writes a furious letter to *The Evening Star* in Washington, DC, calling Joey's trip to America a "foolish and dangerous stunt."

"The germs of the disease are numerous in the mucous secretions," M. M. C. writes. "Joey's sneeze, Joey's cough would spread a shower around. Why in the name of all that is reasonable should we bring a foreign person into this country possibly to afflict some of our own citizens with a dreaded disease of ancient heritage, the cure of which is very long at best, and doubtful and unreliable at worst? When will we outgrow such maudlin sentimentality?"

M. M. C. says the attorney general deserves the "censure of the nation" for allowing Joey to come to the United States.

Stein, editor of *The Star*, prints M. M. C.'s letter. He points out many of its inaccuracies—primarily, the misconception that leprosy travels through the mucous membranes. He also notes that in the fifty-four years that Carville has been in operation, not a single employee has ever contracted Hansen's disease, despite their repeated exposure to patients like Joey, and authorities are convinced that the average adult, even in endemic areas, has natural immunity.

This would ultimately be proved true in 2001, when scientists confirm that 95 percent of the population is naturally immune to leprosy.

One of Joey's supporters, a man named Robert Zeigler, also responds to M. M. C.'s letter. Zeigler emphasizes that the transmission of Hansen's disease is so rare that "none of the American soldiers she fed during the occupation, that she led past minefields into the Battle of Manila, and those she carried, wounded, off the battlefield, has been known to have contracted the disease."

M. M. C.'s letter is just one of many that deride Joey's arrival. But if the dissenters think they will intimidate Joey, they are wrong.

THE UNITED STATES
IN 1948

Japanese Americans were forced to relocate to internment camps at the height
of World War II. Many of them traveled to the camps by train. This photo was
taken in California in 1942.
US National Archives

Joey arrived in the United States in 1948 at a time of national
turmoil. There was rampant post-war inflation, which drove up
the prices of goods and services; the first signs of a Cold War
between the US and the Soviet Union had emerged; and the
fight for civil rights had divided much of the country.

Democratic President Harry S. Truman was running for
reelection on a platform that included federal laws intended

to crack down on lynchings, poll taxes, and employment discrimination. Southern Democrats who supported racial segregation—the separation of Blacks and whites—chafed at Truman's agenda for equal rights. After contentious debates in Congress, these segregationists abandoned their party and created one of their own, called "Dixiecrats." One of the central goals of the Dixiecrats was to keep Blacks out of politics and uphold the white supremacist ideals of segregation. As the Democrats continued to support integration and civil rights, Dixiecrats and other segregationists abandoned the party and joined the Republicans instead.

Asian Americans, particularly Japanese Americans, faced escalating discrimination and racial prejudice during and after World War II. Following the bombing of Pearl Harbor, the American government forcibly removed 120,000 Japanese Americans from their homes and incarcerated them in internment camps. They had committed no crime. They were imprisoned simply for their Japanese ancestry. Nearly seventy thousand were American citizens; many were from families who had lived in the United States for several generations. The prisoners were released in June 1946.

CHAPTER 34

Joey Guerrero is one of the few residents at Carville who isn't using a fake name and false identity. But there is another too—Gertie Hornbostel. As soon as Gertie and Joey swap stories about the war, Gertie comes to an amazing realization: had it not been for Joey's delivery of the minefield map, she would have never been liberated from Santo Tomas internment camp.

"Joey's exploit saved the lives of all those men who were rushing to save us," Gertie later wrote. "At the time we did not realize we owed our lives to this one little Filipina girl."

Like the other residents of Carville, Gertie had anticipated Joey's arrival, but she wasn't aware of their special connection to Santo Tomas. The two women quickly become friends.

Joey and Gertie have other things in common too.

For one, neither of them is easily swayed.

Not only did Gertie maintain her identity, but she brought her husband with her to Carville as well. This was unprecedented at the time, since Hans didn't have Hansen's disease. But Gertie and Hans insisted. Together, they built their own cottage and waited to see what the rest of their lives would bring.

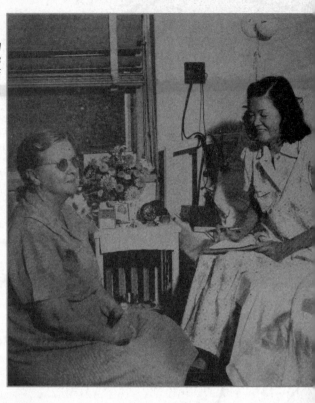

*Gertie Hornbostel and
Joey Guerrero, August 1948*
From the permanent collection of
the National Hansen's Disease Museum,
Carville, Louisiana

*Gertie Hornbostel in the offices
of the Carville Star, late 1940s*
From the permanent collection of the National
Hansen's Disease Museum, Carville, Louisiana

Joey, too, was anxious to discover what lay ahead for her.

"Joey fulfills all our expectations," Gertie says of her friend. "Although sick, she is full of life and smiles, and I know she will accomplish what she has set out to do."

Once upon a time, the path of Joey's life seemed safe and predictable—wife, mother, devoted and obedient Catholic. She was still those things, of course. But the girl who had once pretended to be Joan of Arc had somehow managed to turn make-believe into reality.

While she's at Carville, Joey, an avid reader and writer, plans to finish high school. When asked what she expects of her time in Louisiana, she gives the same answer, again and again: She anticipates she will only be there for two years. Three at most. And then, she says, she will return to the Philippines.

Gertie and Hans Hornbostel at the Carville Post Office, late 1940s
From the permanent collection of the National Hansen's Disease Museum, Carville, Louisana

Joey wakes up every day to attend the six a.m. Mass at the chapel. After Mass, she returns to her room, makes her bed, and writes letters or poetry. At seven thirty, it's time for breakfast. Sometimes she eats in her room, but she usually joins the others in the cafeteria.

Joey enrolls in classes at Carville so she can earn an American high school diploma. Her mornings are spent in class, where she receives high marks. At the end of the school day, she spends her time reading to blind patients, or to those who never learned how to read. She also spends a lot of time reading on her own. Her favorites are biographies or books on travel. Joey has a wanderlust spirit. She even writes a poem imagining all the famous sites of Europe she hopes to see someday.

> I browsed among the masters at the Louvre—
> Took in the fashion shows and even the Follies Bergere
> I thrilled to the gory bullfights in . . . Spain,
> And for a constitutional, a stroll on the Rue de la Paix!
> I sat in ecstatic rapture at the Scala in Milan,

AT LAST SHE STOOD

Loved and lived a lifetime with Puccini's Cho-Cho-San.
Paris in the springtime, I had a rendezvous with Mona Lisa,
Her smile mocked at me like the Leaning Tower of Pisa. . . .

On a pilgrimage to Portugal, I knelt before a shrine,
Out there I was told the angels have a whale of a time!
A tour included a mountain climb to the famous Matterhorn. . . .

Like many countries, France had the great River Seine,
Across her span the Bridge of Sighs all over again.
Germany has her Rhine, through Italy's valleys, the River Po.
Nostalgic memories of muddy Mississippi follow wherever I go.

In addition to literature and poetry, Joey nurtures her love of music. Most of the residents listen to jazz on the radio, but she prefers classical, especially Johannes Brahms, a nineteenth-century German composer known for his beautifully crafted, heartfelt compositions. One of Joey's secret ambitions is to go to all the places where she can listen to music, such as Carnegie Hall in New York.

True to her nature, Joey hardly rests. She takes correspondence courses on fashion design. She spends time learning carpentry and eventually builds her own desk. She volunteers as a secretary for the Patients Federation so she can learn office and secretarial skills. She already speaks two languages—her native Filipino, of course, and English, which was taught to Filipinos during the American occupation—but she wants to learn others.

Joey at her typewriter, 1948
From the permanent collection
of the National Hansen's
Disease Museum, Carville, Louisiana

During this time, Joey receives stacks of letters, including one from Father Julien, who remembers the woman in black who tried to rescue his diary years ago.

CHAPTER 36

Because Joey is less than five feet tall and weighs fewer than a hundred pounds, she is often described as a girl, even though she's a grown woman.

Joey may be small, but her fighting spirit is mighty, and that becomes clear soon after she arrives in Carville.

Joey is outgoing, friendly, and not one to sit quietly. She makes friends easily, and while her routine includes activities like church, school, and volunteerism, she is also incredibly social. She loves to laugh and dance and have fun.

A lifelong devout Catholic, Joey has great respect for the hierarchy of the Catholic Church, so she is devastated when she is suddenly at odds with the priest at Carville, who refuses to give her communion.

When the administrators at Carville ask the priest for an explanation, he tells them that he wants nothing to do with her. He says he doesn't think it's appropriate for her to be friends with any of the men at Carville, because she is married.

"[He] feels that she should confine herself only to the women," the report states. The priest also explains that "he indicated many instances in which he had tried to find out what she was reading

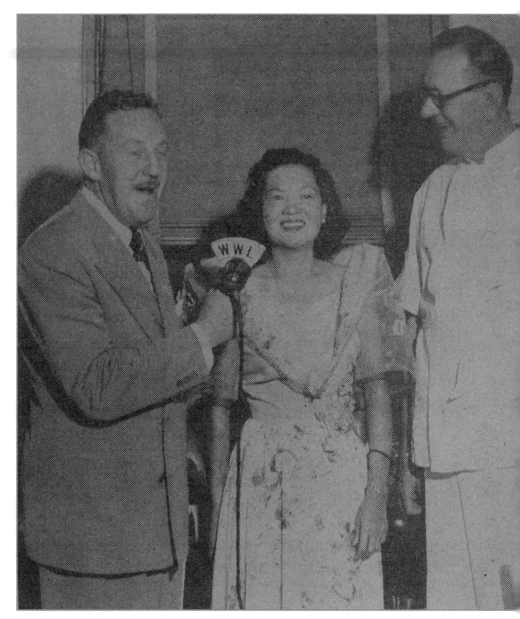

Joey speaks to a radio station about the plight of patients with Hansen's disease, August 1948.
From the permanent collection of the National Hansen's Disease Museum, Carville, Louisiana

and she had refused to show him the title of the book."

When administrators ask Joey about this, she tells them that she doesn't understand the priest's attitude. She explains that she had been taught from childhood to respect priests and what they represent in the Catholic religion, but she is finding it more and more difficult to do so. She says she will find a way to travel to New Orleans for communion if she must, but she is not going to endure mistreatment anymore, even from a priest.

The issue is eventually resolved.

During her long campaign to get to Carville, and during her short time in the United States, Joey has made many friends. In December 1950, Dr. Frederick Johansen, Carville's medical director, gives Joey permission to visit one of those friends in El Paso, Texas, for Christmas. The state health officer of Texas gives clearance too. According to the rules they establish, Joey is allowed to travel to Texas—and only Texas.

Traveling outside of Carville is serious business. Because of their medical condition, patients are not allowed to move freely. They need permission, not only from the medical team at Carville, but from the health officers of every state they pass through. Breaking these rules can create significant backlash for the Carville administration and from the public, who still carry a deep-seated fear of the disease.

But Joey is willing to break the rules to advocate for herself and other people with leprosy. She makes her stop in El Paso, but she also accepts an invitation to speak at a public meeting of the American Legion in Tucson, Arizona, to raise awareness of Hansen's disease. Her visit receives ample publicity. The *Tucson Daily Star* reports on Joey's accomplishments in the Philippines—not just the war effort, but her advocacy on behalf of the "leper colonies" there.

When Dr. Johansen learns of the publicity, he temporarily revokes Joey's travel privileges. If she wants to leave again, he says, she will have to provide a "complete understanding relative to her movements."

The following year, when Joey puts in a request to visit Father F. L. Zimmerman in Saint Louis, Missouri, Dr. Johansen ultimately gives permission, as long as Father Zimmerman agrees to take personal responsibility for all Joey's activities.

"[Joey] is still an active case under treatment and she caused me considerable embarrassment last Christmas," Dr. Johansen writes. "A reliable party had requested that she visit El Paso and Joey had given her word that this would be the extent of her visit. She proceeded from there [to make] personal appearances in Arizona before one or more gatherings, which were given wide newspaper publicity. She had no authority from the State Health Departments in the states through which she passed."

Father Zimmerman vouches for her. Ultimately, Joey's visit to Saint Louis passes without incident, but Dr. Johansen maintains his watchful eye. Just in case.

CHAPTER 37

Joey Guerrero's activism inspires others. George Doody of Mound, Minnesota, for example.

Doody spent four years in a tuberculosis sanatorium and refers to himself as a "lunger"—slang for someone who suffers from a disease of the lungs. After reading about Joey's bravery during the war and her arrival in the US, he's inspired to start a fund drive called Joey's International Leprosy Fund. Doody has no experience in social services or fundraising, but he won't let that stop him.

"I dream big," he writes to Stanley Stein at Carville. Doody explains that he has two objectives: to help those afflicted with leprosy and to raise public awareness of the disease. "I make no promises, for I do not know what lies ahead, in an uncharted sea."

Doody says he would have never considered such an endeavor if not for Joey.

"Polio had its FDR. Leprosy has its Joey," Doody writes, referring to US President Franklin D. Roosevelt, who suffered from polio, but went on to become one of the most popular and revered leaders in the modern world. "The fact that this little [woman] is more than just one of the greatest and most inspiring personalities of our time—

one of those rare humans that crosses the stage of life but once in a blue moon—gave me the courage to try to do what everybody told me was utterly impossible. I am just one of these little people who is putting on a one-man campaign to help the lepers. I am an old 'lunger' and proud of it, and I'd fight the ignorance, superstition, and psychopathic nonsense with a typewriter, as I am now doing, bearing all expense, and I shall continue to do so."

He signs off by saying that his fundraising effort is "my way of saying, thank you, Joey, for what you did to preserve the free way of life . . . during the war. I am very grateful [and] I consider it an honor and great privilege that she permits me to do what I am doing."

Doody donates some of the money from the fund to leprosariums in the Philippines, all in Joey Guerrero's name.

"I am just a simple, ordinary person, not a heroine," Joey wrote to Marie Dachauer in 1945. "I did only what you or any other would have done if called upon to do so. God chose a weak and fragile vessel of clay of the poorest quality when He chose me, but such are the ways of God—they are strange to us poor mortals. . . . I only ask that I love Him with all my heart, all the days of my life, that I remain forever pleasing and beautiful in His sight. That is all I ask, nothing more.

"Someday, my boat will carry me home."

CHAPTER 38

In December 1950, the Underwood Typewriter Company gives Joey a brand-new typewriter. It's well-known that Joey loves to write, and the gift is a symbol of gratitude for all her work during the war.

Joey places her writing desk near the window. She tries to keep the desk tidy, but it is always littered with papers, writing supplies, and letters. Her room at Carville has become her sanctuary, with its soft pastel green walls and sand-colored linoleum floor. Joey loves plants, so she fills her room with them—potted plants sit on the windowsill, ivy and philodendron overflow from hanging pots. She has a dresser with a small mirror and a cabinet with a two-plate burner, record player, and records. An image of the Sacred Heart of Jesus dominates one wall.

One of the first things she writes is an essay about what it means to live in a small, confined community where you interact with the same people every day of your life for years. Being at Carville is not unlike being a kid in school, where "every little thing looms up into huge proportions, where every little fault becomes a mortal sin, where an innocent remark is made into a headline."

It's easy to lose your identity in a place like this, she writes.

"Always [there is] the fear of being misconstrued, the annoyance of being criticized," she writes. "Sometimes, it seems the easiest thing to do is try to create a 'stand-in' personality, one that pleases everyone. . . . After a while, one actually succeeds in a dual role. We are fortunate that we have the privacy of our rooms, where we can retire into our own selves, shedding our stage costumes and paint, forgetting the outer world of make-believe, and even if it is only for the night, of completely shutting out that other self."

This is why she considers her room her sanctum, a place where she is her own true self. Everything in it is an expression of the many facets of herself, including the sides of her that most people don't see.

"This is my castle," she says.

Joey at her new typewriter, with her doll Ah Choo in the background, December 1950
From the permanent collection of the National Hansen's Disease Museum, Carville, Louisiana

CHAPTER 39

Joey Guerrero thought her life in the United States would only last a short while, but each week stretches into the next and she still isn't cured. With each passing day, her desire to return to the Philippines wanes. Joey has increasingly become a voice for advocacy, and her husband back at home isn't happy about it. This—coupled with their long separation—has taken its toll. Although she and her daughter, Cynthia, exchange letters, the ocean between them has slowly turned them into strangers.

Joey's old life is slipping away.

So she focuses on the horizon ahead.

In July 1953, at the age of thirty-six, she slips on a white cap and gown and joins one other patient—eighteen-year-old Bert King, from Florida—for high school commencement. Joey is the valedictorian, having earned all As and Bs, except for a single C in geometry. Bert is the salutatorian by default.

It is raining on the day of Joey's graduation, but the stage at Carville is decorated with flowers and two chaplains are on hand to deliver remarks. Although it's a proud and joyful day for her, it's also racked with uncertainty. Joey has now been at Carville for more

Joey graduates
high school at
Carville in 1953,
at the age of
thirty-six.
From the
permanent
collection of the
National Hansen's
Disease Museum,
Carville, Louisiana

than four years—twice as long as she originally hoped—and her visa, which allows her to stay in the United States, has expired.

A Louisiana Congressman, James Morrison, introduces a bill to the US Congress on March 20, 1951, to intervene on Joey's behalf, but the bill is tabled in favor of other congressional business, and on July 29, 1953, the US Immigration and Naturalization Service holds a deportation hearing to have her sent back to the Philippines. But Joey wants to stay where she is, looking straight ahead at a future in America. The Philippines is still struggling to recover from war, her marriage to Renato is over, and communication with her daughter has broken beneath the weight of separation. Her health, on the other hand, continues to improve under the care of the Carville medical team. She's doing so much better, in fact, that Dr. Johansen allows members of the public—Joey's friends, mostly—to attend her commencement.

The medical treatment at Carville has surpassed many people's expectations overall. In 1945, sulfone drugs became the treatment of choice at Carville, and the results had been promising in the years since. Before sulfone, the main form of treatment was chaulmoogra oil, which produced dubious results and hampered the patients' quality of life. Chaulmoogra oil was known to cause abscesses, nausea, and other complications. But sulfone is another matter. It gives patients hope.

That said, the treatment is imperfect, and there are still many questions to be answered. Although sulfones are successful at arresting the disease in *some* patients, they don't work for *all* patients, and no one knows why. Each month, patients anxiously await their test results to find out if they still have active cases of leprosy. Sometimes they do. Other times, the test comes back negative, only to return positive the following month.

The timing of these tests is important to the patients of Carville, because the clinical rules are clear: Residents may not leave until they receive twelve consecutive negative tests. This means that the negative results must happen twelve times in a row. If you get eleven negatives and one positive, the requirement resets back to square one.

As time goes on and research improves, the reality of consecutive negative tests becomes increasingly attainable. By the time Joey graduates, Gertie Hornsbostel has already passed her screenings and moved with her husband to New York.

Things have also progressed outside the walls of Carville. Leprosy is no longer considered a quarantinable disease by the Louisiana legislature, for example. The stigma certainly hasn't disappeared, but it's fading, bit by bit.

Life for Joey is on an upswing, and she wants to keep it that way. Earning an American high school diploma is just the beginning, as far as she's concerned. But if she's going to succeed in her adopted country—one for which she played such a pivotal wartime role—she'll have to remind them who she is.

Luckily, there are some who have not forgotten.

THE TREATMENT OF
LEPROSY THROUGHOUT HISTORY

Chaulmoogra seeds
Wikimedia Commons

Chaulmoogra oil, which is extracted from seeds of a tropical tree called *Hydnocarpus wightiana*, was used to treat leprosy for centuries, perhaps as early as the 1300s. However, chaulmoogra oil offered limited success.

In the 1940s, a medicine called dapsone was developed at Carville. This medicine, "the miracle of Carville," was a breakthrough in the treatment of Hansen's disease. When the *M. leprae* bacteria became resistant to dapsone in the 1960s, scientists developed a new multidrug regimen, which included dapsone alongside other drugs. The World Health Organization has provided this multidrug therapy worldwide free of cost since 1981, treating about sixteen million people over the past forty years.

The cure for leprosy is now readily available. Today, it is well understood that the disease is not highly contagious; therefore there is no reason to isolate anyone. If the disease is treated quickly, there are no long-term complications.

Around two hundred thousand people are diagnosed with leprosy each year. Most cases of leprosy today are found in Asia, Africa, and South America, with two-thirds of the cases being diagnosed in India. Unfortunately, many people are diagnosed too late to receive effective and available treatment. This makes leprosy one of the world's leading causes of preventable disability.

PART III: Fighter

In October 1953, as the deportation hearings to send Joey back to the Philippines gain momentum, Joey writes an editorial for *The Star*, detailing her uphill battle for citizenship.

The legal aid division of the Baton Rouge Bar Association intervenes on her behalf, and Joey's many supporters flood government offices in protest. Her friends at the American Legion, a nonprofit organization of US war veterans, adopt a resolution on her behalf at their state convention in New Orleans and carry their fight to the national convention, where they bring attention to Joey's unique case.

By now, she says, the horrors of World War II "stand out in a kaleidoscopic pattern in my memory." But two things are vivid: "The grenade-ridden body of my commanding officer [Captain Colayco] who led the First Cavalry into Santo Tomas concentration camp to free the American POWs, and the first plate of pancakes, amber with syrup, which I had not seen for over three years. I longed to eat them, I was so hungry, but my stomach couldn't take it."

This was the plate of food she was served after she delivered the minefield map—the pancakes Captain Blair offered her after

Joey at work in the offices of the Carville Star, *December 1953*
From the permanent collection of the National Hansen's Disease Museum, Carville, Louisiana

expressing his gratitude and awe at her bravery.

When February 1954 comes around, Joey calls it the "month of promise." The deportation hearings are turning in her favor and her health has steadily improved. She moves freely and without pain. Blindness is always a concern with leprosy patients, but her vision is good. She has scars from her longtime battle with skin lesions, but the new sores don't appear as fast or as furiously as they had in the past. Like the other patients at Carville, she submits to monthly tests to determine if the disease is still present or if it's been "arrested"—the term used to describe continued absence of infection. She still tests positive for leprosy, but she feels well, and that's good enough for now.

The efforts of Louisiana Congressman James Morrison, who wrote the 1951 bill in Joey's favor, gain new life. Veteran associations

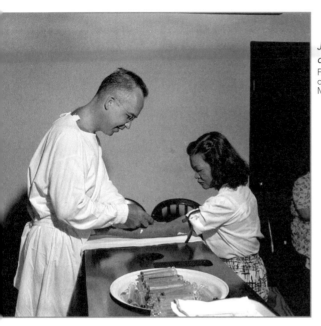

Joey receives care from a doctor at Carville, 1948.
From the permanent collection of the National Hansen's Disease Museum, Carville, Louisiana

across the country adopt resolutions to support the Morrison bill. One such resolution, from the same army division to which Joey delivered the fateful map, states that it fully supports "citizenship for Joey Guerrero, who, by her actions, has demonstrated those traits of Christian brotherhood and service to her fellow men, which citizens of the United States hold supreme."

"It may be a sick world, but it certainly has some lovely and wonderful people in it!" Joey writes for *The Star.* "How could anyone lose?"

Congressman James Morrison of Louisiana makes an impassioned case on Joey's behalf. In his remarks to the US House of Representatives in 1952, he explains that his bill intends to provide permanent residency to "a most distinguished and courageous woman."

He cites an article in *Reader's Digest* from 1951, written by Thomas Johnson, in which a full account of Joey's bravery is outlined.

"[Joey] radiated courage and faith to hollow-eyed GIs, some of whom gave her information they had gleaned from talkative . . . guards," Johnson writes. Johnson describes her actions during the war, but also details all the things Joey did for the patients at Tala, documenting it for perpetuity in the Congressional Record.

"She was instrumental in saving the lives of many Americans and Filipinos. By her outstanding courage and bravery, Mrs. Guerrero made a distinct contribution to the cause of freedom," Representative Morrison states. "I believe that the entire membership of this House will be most interested in seeing that this woman is repaid by our great nation for her heroism, courage, and bravery, by allowing her to become a citizen of the United States, by the favorable enactment of this bill."

Immigration officials agree to drop Joey's case indefinitely, which means they will no longer pursue deportation.

With another conflict won, she is determined to triumph over her longest battle of all: overcoming Hansen's disease.

After nine years—in April 1957—Joey finally achieves twelve consecutive negative swabs for Hansen's disease, and she is allowed to leave Carville. She is thirty-nine years old.

Joey gathers her belongings—typewriter, books, medals, records, her beloved doll—and says goodbye to her friends. Her two-year stay stretched into nearly a decade, and her future is uncertain, but Joey is a fighter. She steps off the grounds of Carville and looks to her life ahead.

She knows it will not be easy.

"I have often been discouraged," Joey said years earlier, when she gave her valedictory address. "I was sick. I was tired. I was disgusted. And there were moments when everything seemed wrong and without purpose. But I told myself that I cannot live forever on the charity of my friends. I must stand on my own two feet. But how? With crutches? With stilts? No.

"I must learn to walk alone."

After Carville, Joey moves to California and lives with friends as she looks for work. She is honest with potential employers about her medical history and anticipates that her road to gainful employment will be marred with "prejudice and bigotry along with disappointments," as she tells a friend.

She is right.

When she reveals to employers that she spent the last ten years in a hospital with Hansen's disease, they look at her "as if I was some ex-criminal," she writes to Eloesser.

Joey has always considered herself a woman of honesty and integrity, but as she's turned away from one interview after another, she decides to invent a new past for herself. At Carville, she was one of the few patients who kept her identity. Now, she wants to shed it. She changes her last name to Leaumax. She will no longer tell the truth about where she's been or what she's done. Unfortunately, her strategy doesn't always work. Sometimes, her employers find out about her diagnosis. She is fired again and again.

At one low point, she is so destitute that she walks into a pawn shop—a store that gives money in exchange for valuables—and pawns her Medal of Freedom.

Finally, she gets a steady office job at Levi Strauss & Co., an American clothing company, where she interacts with the public daily. "All day long buyers and customers complain and insult me because I have an accent," she later tells a friend. The racist abuse from customers is too much for Joey. She finds work as a secretary to a vice president at a big bank, then becomes a librarian at an engineering company, where she is paid a decent salary for the first time.

In 1965—eight years after being discharged from Carville—Joey enrolls at San Francisco State College, where she majors in English and minors in Spanish. She is forty-seven years old. All her classmates are eighteen, nineteen, and twenty.

Freshman year is hard, but she makes it through.

In late 1967, the US government, taking into consideration all her services during the war, finally grants her something much more permanent than residency: citizenship. She gives an interview to the *San Francisco Chronicle* in honor of the historic moment.

It would be her last.

In the interview, she shares memories of Japanese soldiers, some of whom were kind to her.

"They would show me pictures of their wife and children . . . and there I was, sending them to their deaths," she says. "In those times it was necessary. I really don't like to talk of it. I have almost forgotten."

When the reporter asks about her journey with the minefield map, during which she hid from snipers, was pursued by river pirates, and suffered under the weight of illness and fatigue, she says simply: "They gave me the map and told me to deliver it . . . so I took it there."

In June 1969, Joey graduates from college and is accepted into graduate school at Middlebury College, where she earns a master's degree in Spanish literature. She then spends four years in Niger, Colombia, and El Salvador as a Peace Corps volunteer, teaching children and adults how to read and speak English. She also teaches music and drawing.

When she returns to the United States, she moves to Washington, DC, and works as an usher for the Kennedy Center, where she attends concerts for free.

Finally, Joey can hear all the symphonies she wants.

WHAT IS THE
PEACE CORPS?

The Peace Corps is a United States volunteer organization created by President John F. Kennedy in 1961. The mission of the Peace Corps is to promote world peace by sending trained volunteers to countries that need them.

To join the Peace Corps, you must be at least eighteen years old, in good health, and a US citizen. Volunteers are trained for about three months before they are sent overseas for twenty-four months of service in several sectors. Some work in agriculture to help create sustainable farms. Others teach English, literacy, math, or science in schools and communities. There are volunteers in health education and service, community leadership, and household economic security. Over two hundred thousand Peace Corps volunteers have served in 139 countries.

It is June 1996. Joey Guerrero is seventy-eight years old. She has retired from her most recent job as a bank secretary and has dedicated much of her time as a volunteer usher at the Kennedy Center for the Performing Arts in Washington, DC. The Kennedy Center sits on the banks of the Potomac River. There is a grand foyer with sixteen hand-blown crystal chandeliers, red carpeting, and enormous corridors that are more than sixty feet high. Ushers work mostly at night, guiding patrons to their seats in the sprawling concert hall. When the theater lights fall, Joey focuses on the stage and listens to the music she's always loved. But she no longer needs a record player or her imagination—it's all right here in front of her.

In the last season of her life, the Kennedy Center presents operas by Giuseppe Verdi, Wolfgang Mozart, and Jules Massenet. One of their productions, *Mefistofele* by Arrigo Boito, begins and ends with a heavenly chorus of angels praising God the Creator.

When Joey Guerrero dies of heart failure on June 18, none of the people in her life know anything about her past. Her obituary identifies her as "a retired secretary who had worked as an usher." There is nothing about the extraordinary life she lived. This little girl who played make-believe, who wanted to serve her faith and walk through battlefields like Joan of Arc, had survived war, sickness, and separation. But she hadn't just survived. She was driven by faith, curiosity, and imagination. She received medals, became an advocate, reinvented herself, graduated from college among students half her age, then settled down for a quieter life, one that wasn't beset with hardships of the past, until her ship carried her home. But none of that appears in the newspaper announcement—just the date of her death and the fact that she worked as a secretary and usher.

The obituary states that she has no immediate survivors, but of course, that is not true. When Joey dies, her daughter, Cynthia, is alive across the ocean in the Philippines, now caring for her own children. Cynthia has conflicted feelings about her mother—she understands that Joey was forced down an unexpected path because of her illness, but she also feels abandoned, and sorrowful that they lived separate lives. Cynthia was able to visit her mother before she died, but they never truly reconnected.

When Joey's friends gather the belongings in her modest apartment, they discover a few record albums, many autographed theater and ballet posters, and nearly nine hundred books.

There is no evidence of her past life as a spy, wife, mother, or leprosy patient. It is discovered that she left strict orders at Carville that her whereabouts be kept secret. Many friends she'd made throughout her early years in the US don't know how to find her. They send letters that are left unanswered.

There are some exceptions, however. Like Dr. Eloesser, the tuberculosis specialist. He is the friend she confides in about the racism and challenges she faced after leaving Carville. She sends him a long letter with a photograph.

"Most people think I have died because I have tried very hard to efface the past," she writes. "I simply want to forget it. It was too traumatic and has given me no end of heartbreak. [But] I am still alive and full of zest for life."

Among her files at Carville is this note:

I have overcome my hurts, my griefs,
my disenchantment, and out of seeming despair
I learned to cope, to rise up, to learn new and
exciting things amongst the doubts and the turmoil.
I've traveled a long, tortured road and left the past
where it belongs.
That book of my life is over.

Students often ask where I get my ideas. If they could peek inside my brain, they wouldn't have to ask. My mind is a busy place, crowded with never-ending stories. I think of stories when I drive. I think of stories when I get the mail. I think of stories when I cook dinner, do the dishes, watch TV. They almost always develop from my imagination. I'm rarely inspired by events of real life.

This book is an exception.

It started with an event hosted by Browseabout Books in Rehoboth Beach, Delaware, featuring Pam Fessler, the author of *Carville's Cure: Leprosy, Stigma, and the Fight for Justice*. The Carville leprosarium—now known as the National Hansen's Disease Museum—was just two hours' drive from my hometown. I attended the event, bought the book, and started reading. I've long had an interest in infectious diseases but didn't know much about leprosy. I was intrigued.

When I reached page 199, I sat up straight, eyes wide in wonder. That's the moment I met Joey Guerrero.

So began the journey of *At Last She Stood*.

I was so eager to get Joey's story into the hands of young readers, I didn't give much thought to *how* I would do it. I'd been a journalist for more than ten years—how hard could it be?

Quite hard, it turns out.

Writing this book was like working a puzzle with half the pieces missing. The names of her parents and how they died are lost to us. She had a brother, but his name is unknown, as is his fate. There is very little about her childhood or schooling. Even after she arrives in the United States and the records become more robust, there are still question marks. We know, for example, that Joey married a fellow patient at Carville named Alex Lau, but there is virtually no information about their marriage, how it ended, or why.

There were many nights when I desperately wished Joey had left behind a journal, diaries, huge stacks of letters, *something* to answer the never-ending list of questions I had about her life. But writing is never easy, no matter what.

During my research, I read dozens of books, scoured through hundreds of issues of Carville's newspaper, *The Star*, mined the National Archives for weeks, visited Carville, walked the same halls as Joey. I connected with librarians and Jesuits in the Philippines, spoke to Manny Guerrero, one of Joey's living relatives, and attended classes on World War II taught by historian John Fulgoney through the Osher Lifelong Learning Institute at the University of Delaware.

The research process was arduous and often frustrating. But I kept Joey close through it all—staring at her picture, wondering what questions I would ask if she were sitting across from me, hoping she'd be proud of the work I was doing.

As an author, my goal—always—is to honor and respect the people I write about, whether real or fictional.

It is my hope that Joey feels that honor on these pages, wherever she may be. And that you are intrigued and inspired by her story, as I am.

ACKNOWLEDGMENTS

I am deeply indebted to Elizabeth Schexnayder with the National Hansen's Disease Museum in Carville, Louisiana. I also owe great appreciation to numerous librarians, researchers, and historians in the United States and the Philippines, including Abraham Ignacio, Alley Horn, John Fulgoney, and Kelsey Madges, and early supporters of Joey's story, especially Sharon Huss Roat, Dan Eaker, Sara Crowe, and the entire team at Greenwillow Books, specifically Virginia Duncan, Mikayla Lawrence, and Shannah Harris. Thank you, Sylvie Le Floc'h and Anna and Elena Balbusso, for this beautiful cover.

Much gratitude to fellow authors Sawyer Lovett, Claire Rudolph Murphy, and Betty Ann Quirino, and to the Filipino School of New York and New Jersey, especially Venessa G. Manzano and Noel Pangilinan. Thank you, Manny Guerrero, for your time, kindness, and support.

Finally: thank you to my mother, Virgilia, who helped me research, read early drafts, and cheered me along the way. Mahal kita.

FURTHER RESOURCES

- "Bataan Death March" by History.com
  www.history.com/topics/world-war-ii/bataan-death-march

- *Bomb: The Race to Build—and Steal—the World's Most Dangerous Weapon* by Steve Sheinkin—a nonfiction book about the building of the atomic bomb

- Bulosan Center for Filipino Studies / Welga Digital Archive—includes oral histories about the Filipino-American experience
  https://welgadigitalarchive.omeka.net/

- Densho—a website with documented testimonies, lesson plans, and discussion questions related to the forced removal of Japanese Americans from their homes into US internment camps
  https://densho.org/about-densho/

- *Every Ounce of Courage: A Daughter's Reflection on Her Mother's Bravery* by Elizabeth Ann Besa-Quirino—the story of Lulu Reyes

- The Filipino Veterans Recognition and Education Project
  https://filvetrep.org/

- "From Outcast to Spy to Outcast: The War Hero with Hansen's Disease" by Lea Schram van Haupt, National World War II Museum
  www.nationalww2museum.org/war/articles/philippines-spy-joey-guerrero

- Holocaust Encyclopedia, United States Holocaust Memorial Museum
  https://encyclopedia.ushmm.org/

- The Leprosy Mission
  www.leprosymission.org

- "Mrs Guerrero—Heroine of Filipino Underground," posted by British Pathé—a newsreel of Joey's arrival
www.youtube.com/watch?v=Na4l6BSrM8I

- The National Hansen's Disease Museum (formerly known as Carville Leprosarium)
www.hrsa.gov/hansens-disease/museum

- "World War II: Asian Pacific American Perspectives," compiled by Colorín Colorado—a booklist
www.colorincolorado.org/booklist/world-war-ii-asian-pacific-american-perspectives

NOTES

Front flap
"my quiet war": Johnson, "Joey's Quiet War," 47.

Back cover
"I have often been discouraged. . . .": Montgomery, *The Leper Spy*, 215.

EPIGRAPHS

"I am just a simple, ordinary person . . .": Guerrero, Letter to Marie Dachauer.
"I went globe-trotting across the hemisphere . . .": Guerrero, "Wunderlust," 11.

PART I: SPY

Chapter 4
"racial enemies": United States Holocaust Memorial Museum, "Victims of the Nazi Era: Nazi Racial Ideology."

Chapter 5
"I don't know anything about propaganda work. . . .": Terami-Wada, "The Japanese Propaganda Corps in the Philippines," 283.

Chapter 8
"Pauvre, pauvre.": Julien and Pezdirtz, *Promises Kept*, 29.

Chapter 9
"strange, hidden life": Guerrero, Letter to Marie Dachauer.
"Are you Padre Julien?": Julien and Pezdirtz, *Promises Kept*, 30–31.

Chapter 10
"Why do you still allow yourselves to be the slaves . . .": Terami-Wada, "The Japanese Propaganda Corps in the Philippines," 294.

Chapter 13
"Do you have anything you shouldn't have? . . . Do you have a Mama?": Julien and Pezdirtz, *Promises Kept*, 43–44.

Chapter 15
"Come to our house.": Johnson, "Joey's Quiet War," 47.

"A woman of your spirit should join the guerrillas.": Johnson, "Joey's Quiet War,"
47.

"You're the kind for our secret service. . . .": Johnson, "Joey's Quiet War," 47.

Chapter 17

*"If I don't run risks, I won't find out anything worthwhile. . . . nothing inside worth
looking at":* Monaghan, *Under the Red Sun*, 259–60.

Chapter 18

"People of the Philippines . . .": MacArthur, "World War II Speech."

"Just tell me where to go.": Johnson, "Joey's Quiet War," 47.

"little errand boy": Monaghan, *Under the Red Sun*, 260.

Chapter 20

"They'll be back in ten days.": Julien and Pezdirtz, *Promises Kept*, 53.

Chapter 21

"Where is the map?": Monaghan, *Under the Red Sun*, 265.

Chapter 22

"I wonder what that is.": Julien and Pezdirtz, *Promises Kept*, 73.

"will have the fortune of receiving the greatest honor . . .": Scott, *Rampage*, 138.

Chapter 24

"Novaliches—I keep repeating the word to myself. . . .": Monaghan, *Under the
Red Sun*, 268.

"There is pity for every other disease. . . ." Monaghan, *Under the Red Sun*, 269.

Chapter 25

*"God must have some special work for you to do among those poor forsaken
creatures. . . .":* Monaghan, *Under the Red Sun*, 269.

"Consider that you are going to an austere cloister . . .": Monaghan, *Under the
Red Sun*, 270.

PART II: SURVIVOR

Chapter 26

"Marie is interested in helping lepers all over the world. . . .": Guerrero, Letter to
Marie Dachauer.

Chapter 27

"Dear Miss Marie . . . our fairy godmother.": Guerrero, Letter to Marie Dachauer.

Chapter 28

"a graveyard of the living dead . . . The children, in particular, look up to her.":
Montgomery, *The Leper Spy*, 153.

Chapter 29
"There is so much to do, so many things to accomplish and time is short. . . .": Guerrero, Letter to Dr. Leo Eloesser, September 30.

Chapter 30
"cross-section of the all the world's races and nationalities": Stein and Blochman, *Alone No Longer,* 61.

Chapter 31
"I'm a better sailor than flier. . . . The nuns are gentle and talk in soft voices.": Guerrero, Letter to Dr. Frederick Johansen.
"I am finally here. . . . I am in America.": Guerrero, "First Impressions," 1–2.

Chapter 32
"Here we are, Joey. . . . Look at all this luxury!": Guerrero, "First Impressions," 1–2.

Chapter 33
"a foolish and dangerous stunt . . .": M. M. C., "Disapproves Joey's Trip."
"none of the American soldiers she fed during the occupation, that she led past minefields . . .": Zeigler, "Joey's Patron Explains the Cause."

Chapter 34
"Joey's exploit saved the lives of all those men who were rushing to save us. . . .": Hornbostel, "As I See It," 3–4.
"Joey fulfills all our expectations. . . .": Hornbostel, "As I See It," 4.

Chapter 35
"I browsed among the masters at the Louvre . . .": Guerrero, "Wunderlust," 11.

Chapter 36
"[He] feels that she should confine herself only to the women. . . .": Reebel, "Case of Mrs. Josephine Guerrero: Case No. 1957."
"a complete understanding relative to her movements" and *"[Joey] is still an active case under treatment and she caused me considerable embarrassment last Christmas. . . .":* Johansen, Letter to Assistant Surgeon General R. C. Williams.

Chapter 37
"I dream big. . . .": Doody, Letter to Stanley Stein.
"Polio had its FDR. Leprosy has its Joey. . . .": Doody, Letter to Stanley Stein.
"I am just a simple, ordinary person, not a heroine. . . .": Guerrero, Letter to Marie Dachauer.

Chapter 38
"every little thing looms up into huge proportions . . . This is my castle.": Guerrero, "Home Away from Home," 9.

PART III: FIGHTER

Chapter 40

"stand out in a kaleidoscopic pattern in my memory . . . month of promise": Guerrero, "Jottings," 9.

"citizenship for Joey Guerrero, who, by her actions . . .": Morrison, Congressional Record (1952) 207412-43228.

"It may be a sick world . . .": Guerrero, "Jottings," 9.

"a most distinguished and courageous woman": Morrison, Congressional Record (1952) 207412-43228.

"[Joey] radiated courage and faith . . .": Johnson, "Joey's Quiet War," 47.

"She was instrumental . . .": Morrison, Congressional Record (1952) 207412-43228.

Chapter 41

"I have often been discouraged. . . .": Montgomery, *The Leper Spy*, 215.

"prejudice and bigotry along with disappointments . . . because I have an accent.": Guerrero, Letter to Dr. Leo Eloesser, September 25.

"They would show me pictures of their wife and children . . . so I took it there.": Montgomery, *The Leper Spy*, 248.

Chapter 42

"Most people think I have died . . .": Guerrero, Letter to Dr. Leo Eloesser, September 25.

"I have overcome my hurts, my griefs, my disenchantment . . .": Guerrero, Note at Carville.

Besa-Quirino, Elizabeth Ann. *Every Ounce of Courage: A Daughter's Reflection on Her Mother's Bravery*. Published by the author, 2023.

Brittanica Kids. "World War II." Accessed September 3, 2024. https://kids.britannica.com/kids/article/World-War-II/353934.

Budge, Kent G. "Ishikawa Shingo (1889-1947)." The Pacific War Online Encyclopedia, 2013–14. http://pwencycl.kgbudge.com/I/s/Ishikawa_Shingo.htm.

Centers for Disease Control and Prevention. "About Hansen's Disease (Leprosy)." Published April 11, 2024. www.cdc.gov/leprosy/.

Central Luzon Leprosarium, Tala, Novaliches. Leprosy Clinical Record. November 5, 1945.

Condon-Rall, Mary Ellen. "U.S. Army Medical Preparations and the Outbreak of War: The Philippines, 1941-6 May 1942." *The Journal of Military History* 56, no. 1 (1992): 35–36.

Doody, George. Letter to Stanley Stein. September 19, 1949.

Fessler, Pam. *Carville's Cure: Leprosy, Stigma, and the Fight for Justice*. Liveright Publishing Corporation, 2020.

Gould, Tony. *A Disease Apart: Leprosy in the Modern World*. St. Martin's Press, 2005.

Greenfield, Jeff. "A Southern Rebellion in 1948 Almost Threw American Democracy into Disarray." *Politico*, September 24, 2023. www.politico.com/news/magazine/2023/09/24/closest-calls-presidential-upset-1948-00114521.

Grzybowski, Andrzej, and Małgorzata Nita. "Leprosy in the Bible." *Clinics in Dermatology* 34, no. 1 (2016): 429.

Guerrero, Joey. "A Day Around the Clock." *The Star* 11, no. 6 (1952).

Guerrero, Joey. "First Impressions." *The Star* 7, no. 11 (1948): 1–2.

Guerrero, Joey. "Home Away from Home." *The Star* 10, no. 4 (1950): 9.

Guerrero, Joey. "Jottings." *The Star* 13, no. 6 (1954): 9.

Guerrero, Joey. Letter to Dr. Frederick Johansen. July 1948.

Guerrero, Joey. Letter to Dr. Leo Eloesser. September 25, 1970.

Guerrero, Joey. Letter to Dr. Leo Eloesser. September 30, 1947.

Guerrero, Joey. Letter to Marie Dachauer. August 1945.

Guerrero, Joey. "Wunderlust." *The Star* 13, no. 4 (1953): 11.

Herrera, Dana R. "The Philippines: An Overview of the Colonial Era." *Education About Asia: Online Archives* 20, no. 1 (2015): 14–19.

History.com Editors. "General MacArthur Returns to the Philippines." Updated October 17, 2019. www.history.com/this-day-in-history/macarthur-returns.

Hornbostel, Gertrude. "As I See It." *The Star* 7, no. 9 (1948): 3–4.

Hornbostel, Gertrude. "Three Christmases at Sto. Tomas." *The Star* 6, no. 4. (1946): 1–3.

Johansen, F. A. Letter to Assistant Surgeon General R. C. Williams. September 25, 1950.

Johnson, Thomas M. "Joey's Quiet War." *Reader's Digest* 59, no. 352 (1951): 47.

Julien, Fred, and Richard Pezdirtz. *Promises Kept: Memoirs of a Missionary Priest.* Pez-Tex Pub, 1996.

Kalisch, Philip A. "The Strange Case of John Early: A Study of the Stigma of Leprosy" *International Journal of Leprosy* 40, no. 3 (1972): 291–305.

Kendrick, Alexander. "Philippines a Barrier Across Japan's Path." *Philadelphia Inquirer,* December 8, 1941.

Kiyoshi, Miki. "Miki Kiyoshi." In *Sourcebooks for Modern Japanese Philosophy: Selected Documents.* Translated and edited by David A. Dilworth and Valdo H. Viglielmo, with Augustin Jacinto Zavala. Greenwood Press, 1998.

Kratz, Jessie. "Japanese American Internment: Righting a Wrong." US National Archives, February 17, 2017. https://prologue.blogs.archives.gov/2017/02/17/apologizing -for-japanse-internment-righting-a-wrong/.

Labrador, Juan. "Diary of Juan Labrador, O. P.: February 20, 1945." Philippine Diary Project. Accessed September 3, 2024. https://philippinediaryproject.com/1945/02 /20/february-20-1945/.

Lent, John. "Guerrilla Press of the Philippines, 1941-45." *Asian Studies* 41, no. 2 (2005): 116–130.

M. M. C. "Disapproves Joey's Trip." *The Evening Star,* July 27, 1948.

MacArthur, Douglas. "World War II Speech, 'I Have Returned.'" Vincent Voice Library, Michigan State University, 1944. https://catalog.lib.msu.edu/Record/folio .in00004194668.

Milne, Andrea Elizabeth. "We Are No Peculiar Breed of Femmes: Domesticity as Counter-Discourse for Women with Leprosy, 1940-1960." *Frontiers: A Journal of Women Studies* 39, no. 3 (2018): 118–151.

Mitchell, M., and Domingues, Francisco Contente. "Ferdinand Magellan." *Britannica,* July 24, 2024. www.britannica.com/biography/Ferdinand-Magellan.

Monaghan, Forbes J. *Under the Red Sun: A Letter from Manila.* The Declan X. McMullen Company, 1946.

Montgomery, Ben. *The Leper Spy: The Story of an Unlikely Hero of World War II.* Chicago Review Press, 2017.

Moralina, Aaron Rom O. "State, Society, and Sickness: Tuberculosis Control in the American Philippines, 1910-1918." *Philippine Studies* 57, no. 2 (2009): 179–218.

Morley, Ian. "Manila." *Cities* 72, Part A (2018): 17–33.

Morrison, Rep. James H., speaking on Joey Guerrero. 82nd Congress, 2nd sess., Congressional Record (1952) 207412-43228.

National Geographic Kids. "Ten Facts About World War 2." Accessed September 3, 2024. www.natgeokids.com/uk/discover/history/general-history/world-war-two/.

Nish, Ian Hill. *Japanese Foreign Policy in the Interwar Period.* Praeger Publishers, 2002.

Philippine Statistics Authority. "Religious Affiliation in the Philippines." Published February 22, 2023. https://psa.gov.ph/content/religious-affiliation-philippines -2020-census-population-and-housing.

Reebel, Katherine. "Case of Mrs. Josephine Guerrero: Case No. 1957." Carville Social Work Notes, August 29, 1949.

Rizzo, Johnna. "Joan of Arc: The Teenage Girl Who Helped Lead a French Army to Victory." National Geographic Kids. Accessed September 3, 2024. https://kids .nationalgeographic.com/history/article/joan-of-arc.

Sarmiento, Jahzeel, Kristine Gail R. Riego, and Maria Azela L. Tamayo. "Huntahan: Banahaw Mysticism, Urban Legends, and Folktales." *Boletin de Literatura Oral* 10, no. 1 (2023): 2045–2055.

Schons, Mary. "Peace Corps." National Geographic Society, October 19, 2023. https:// education.nationalgeographic.org/resource/peace-corps/.

Scott, James M. *Rampage: MacArthur, Yamashita, and the Battle of Manila.* W.W. Norton, 2018.

"Shooting of Lepers in China," *Leprosy Review* 3, no. 2 (1937):129–30.

Stein, Stanley, with Lawrence G. Blochman. *Alone No Longer: The Story of a Man Who Refused to Be One of the Living Dead!.* Funk & Wagnalls Co., 1963.

Terami-Wada, Motoe. "The Japanese Propaganda Corps in the Philippines." *Philippine Studies* 38, no. 3 (1990): 279–300.

Tharoor, Ishaan. "Manila Was Known as the Pearl of the Orient. Then World War II Happened." *The Washington Post,* February 19, 2015.

Time. "National Affairs: Where Thou Lodgest . . ." *Time Magazine* 47, no. 21 (1946). https://time.com/archive/6773253/national-affairs-where-thou-lodgest/.

"To Rid the Scourge of Leprosy." *South Bend Tribune,* July 26, 1925.

United States Holocaust Memorial Museum. "Victims of the Nazi Era: Nazi Racial Ideology." Holocaust Encyclopedia. https://encyclopedia.ushmm.org/content/en /article/victims-of-the-nazi-era-nazi-racial-ideology.

Vale, M. G. A., and Yvonne Lanhers. "St. Joan of Arc." *Britannica,* July 22, 2024. www.britannica.com/biography/Saint-Joan-of-Arc.

Zeigler, Robert L. "Joey's Patron Explains the Cause." *The Evening Star,* July 30, 1948.